WHAT'S THE MATTER WITH MEAT?

FOOD CONTROVERSIES

SERIES EDITOR: ANDREW F. SMITH

Everybody eats. Yet few understand the importance of food in our lives and the decisions we make each time we eat. The Food Controversies series probes problems created by the industrial food system and examines proposed alternatives.

Already published:

Fast Food: The Good, the Bad and the Hungry Andrew F. Smith
What's So Controversial about Genetically Modified Food? John T. Lang
What's the Matter with Meat? Katy Keiffer

WHAT'S THE MATTER WITH MEAT?

KATY KEIFFER

REAKTION BOOKS

Published by Reaktion Books Ltd
Unit 32, Waterside
44–48 Wharf Road
London N1 7UX, UK

www.reaktionbooks.co.uk

First published 2017

Printed and bound in Great Britain by Bell & Bain, Glasgow

A catalogue record for this book is available from the British Library
ISBN 978 1 78023 760 2

CONTENTS

INTRODUCTION 7
1 THE EVOLUTION OF INDUSTRIALIZED MEAT PRODUCTION 11
2 THE BUSINESS OF GENETICS 27
3 LIVESTOCK AND DISEASE 38
4 ENVIRONMENTAL COSTS 58
5 ANIMAL WELFARE 72
6 WAGES, WORKERS AND SAFETY ISSUES 92
7 CONCENTRATION AND CONSOLIDATION IN THE INDUSTRY 104
8 FOOD FRAUD 116
9 TRADE DEALS AND LAND GRABS 132
10 ASIA AND THE INDUSTRIALIZED MODEL OF MEAT PRODUCTION 143
CONCLUSION 160

REFERENCES 169
BIBLIOGRAPHY 179
ACKNOWLEDGEMENTS 197
INDEX 199

INTRODUCTION

Why has meat become such a contentious food group? It is indisputably popular in most of the world. We certainly eat enough of it. In fact, worldwide, some 315 million tonnes were produced in 2014. That averages out at 43.4 kg per person.[1] And many people don't eat meat at all, so some of us ate even more than our share. Shouldn't we all be thrilled at the rich and plentiful supply of nutritious animal protein that is readily available in so much of the world?

With this astonishing abundance of meat production, quite a few of us have got used to paying next to nothing for it too. For many of us in the West, it is available economically as a daily choice. Developing countries are acquiring their own appetite for meat, often abandoning rice- or plant-based diets in favour of animal protein. In fact, meat consumption has never been higher than it is now, and production is more than keeping up with demand. Between 1970 and 2008, beef production doubled, poultry increased sixfold and pork tripled.[2]

Though statistics show the demand for meat is flattening for Westerners, the newcomers to the meat party are more than making up for any regional losses suffered by the industry. The United Nations projects that we will be producing and consuming nearly 450 million tonnes of meat per year by 2050, roughly double the amount for the year 2000.[3]

Despite the huge production figures, much of the global meat supply is controlled by just a few companies: JBS and Brasil Foods in South America and, in the USA, Tyson Foods, Cargill and Smithfield, now known as the WH Group and Chinese-owned. Certainly there are many others trying to compete with them around the world, but these few companies exemplify how the industry is rapidly transforming into multinational mega-agribusinesses. The desire for meaty meals has been vastly encouraged by fast-food purveyors who lead the way in providing cheap, protein-based options to virtually every nation on earth. It seems that everyone has learned to love burgers and nuggets.

Over the course of the last five decades, the meat industry has adopted ever more dazzling strategies to satisfy the world's craving for low-cost proteins. Indeed, a review of websites, brochures and trade publications could lead one to believe that meat providers stand alone when it comes to generating sufficient quantities of food to meet the demands of the world's burgeoning population, expected to reach more than nine billion by 2050. They routinely portray themselves as shouldering the burden of 'feeding the world' more than any other agricultural sector, conveying an urgent sense that unless we produce enough meat for every person on the planet, we will starve to death in short order. To succeed they will leave no strategy untested, no opportunity to expand unexplored. What's more, they are making astonishing amounts of money in their quest to feed the world. In 2014 JBS, the major player in the world arena, realized a net profit of U.S.$560,279,580.[4]

Tyson posted higher than expected earnings in the first quarter of 2016, showing a staggering profit of U.S.$461 million.[5] *In three months.* One could go on listing the phenomenal sums being coined from raising livestock, except that the people who are doing the raising aren't the ones cashing in.

One must admire the extraordinary ingenuity of the industry when it comes to producing billions of kilograms of meat on less feed and land than any farmer of yesteryear could ever have envisaged. But in the celebratory atmosphere of commercial success, no one anticipated that producing all that meat would also deliver tremendous hidden costs that have been cleverly passed on by the industry in a breathtaking sleight of hand. Those costs include, at the very least, the profound degradation of soil and water; the production of climate-warming air pollution and greenhouse gases; and a steep decline in wages in the sector, accompanied by erosion of basic labour laws. Meanwhile, meat companies and their ancillary industries, feed and pharmaceutical companies, are reaping unheard-of profits. The swallowing of small companies by larger ones has resulted in a near-total absence of competition. Essentially the world has been divvied up into territories, and the companies best suited to each market have monopolized those areas.

From these introductory paragraphs it might be assumed that the author is no fan of meat-eating, but that would be incorrect. Meat is unarguably a nutritious food, providing essential building blocks for healthy growth. Its absence from a diet, while certainly not deadly, does deprive the body of vitamins, minerals, proteins and amino acids that are difficult to replicate in a plant-based diet. Meat is an efficient source of nutrients and, most importantly, is a highly flavourful and versatile component of the diet that makes eating pleasurable. Humans are omnivorous. Our ancestors did not have access to daily rations of meat, but they surely craved it. Much of early man's time was devoted to hunting for animals to eat, and even to this day in tribal populations a kill is a cause to celebrate and to feast. So no, this is not a polemic about how we should not eat meat.

Instead, the object of this book is to explore how the meat industry has increasingly disconnected itself from traditional agriculture and now poses a very real threat to the population it claims to be so anxious to serve, if not save. It is the author's hope that it will inspire consumers to send a clear signal to corporate leaders that the current system is no longer acceptable and will not be supported. Like any other business, the meat industry is profit-driven. Meat companies can and will change their practices as the market demands. It is up to all of us to alert them to what we require as consumers and as world citizens.

Though there are some encouraging signs of change in the meat industry, without continuous pressure from consumers, it will be largely cosmetic. Choosing carefully what to spend money on is one way, but more importantly, consumers must participate in political action to rein in the industry through supporting vigorous labour protections, strict environmental regulation and powerful antitrust legislation. As the industry stretches into new territory, it must be prevented from the egregious practices explored in this book. It is supremely ironic that the food industry could eventually be the industry that not only fails to feed us but contributes the most to the degradation of the planet. We must not let that happen.

1
THE EVOLUTION OF INDUSTRIALIZED MEAT PRODUCTION

For most of history meat has been the food humans are most grateful for. In *Catching Fire: How Cooking Made Us Human*, author Richard Wrangham shows that when we learned to cook meat, we began the transition from ape to man. Small wonder the meat industry has become the world power it is now. And make no mistake, it is a world power. Raising meat as we now do has changed the face of agriculture, pushing us into a new model of 'monocropping' great swathes of land in order to produce food not for people, but for animals. As we will see later in the book, growing these crops and aggregating animals as we do has resulted in never before seen effects on land, water and air. Others argue that eating as much meat as is now consumed has had negative effects on public health. In short, a host of significant problems, ancillary to the business of growing livestock on an industrial scale, are having impacts that no one could have foreseen a hundred years ago when the industry started to ramp up.

Global consumption patterns have gone through enormous changes in just the last five decades. Export trade, improved agricultural methods for growing animal feed, changes in popular culture and other factors have contributed to these massive shifts in the social fabric as it relates to food. What really galvanized the industry was the implementation of the Concentrated Animal Feeding Operation, the much-maligned CAFO. CAFOs have made possible the steady supply of cheap meat that so many of us take for granted.

Concentrated Animal Feeding Operations are factories, not farms. Farmers and ranchers may supply CAFOs with young animals, but then the animals are aggregated in paddocks or, in the cases of pork and poultry, into large warehouses. Carefully mixed food and water are dispensed. That food is typically a mix of grains, oilseeds and cereals combined with hay, or other fodder, and topped off with a cocktail of chemicals formulated to encourage growth and prevent disease. CAFOs are enormously efficient, a trait businessmen and farmers alike can appreciate. Many of the operations are mechanized, keeping labour costs down. Feed is mixed in big silos and then distributed by lorry to conveyor belts in paddocks or feeding stations. The amount the animals eat is carefully calibrated to their growth patterns and they grow quickly, which means that less food and water is required to achieve slaughter weight. Fewer humans have to take care of them – there is no herding, no predators to worry about, no concern about animals wandering off, or being stolen or injured. Compared to traditional farming, who wouldn't adopt this model to produce meat?

We can all thank the United States of America, the land of innovation, for the invention of the CAFO. Contrary to common belief, CAFOs got their start in the poultry industry in the 1930s. Most people think of cattle, squeezed into tiny paddocks, when they think of a CAFO, but in fact it was poultry producers who paved the way. Chickens were once considered a seasonal food. They were raised for eggs, and most rural families had a few birds. The current ubiquitous popularity of chicken on the dinner table is a relatively new phenomenon. Seventy-five years ago chicken was a Sunday supper treat. In the USA it was a Fourth of July, fried chicken celebration. But once vitamins were discovered and, more importantly, could be synthesized into edible form, that pattern changed. People realized that if they fed their chickens vitamin D they could be housed indoors all year round and would continue to lay eggs. This meant an ever-ready supply of fryers and broilers. A few really smart people, like Jesse Jewell (1902–1975), who started as a Georgia feed, seed and fertilizer supplier, worked out that they could put hundreds of chickens at a time indoors to increase profit. Once Jewell had the supply, he set about creating demand by driving his chickens around, pre-slaughtered, packed on ice, and selling them into city butcher shops and restaurants. Around the same time, John Tyson was raising and selling his birds. A few years later, he would start selling chicks to guys like Jesse Jewell, and then grinding the feed to go with them. It would be the beginning of an empire that now stretches around the world.

In the USA the Jewell and Tyson models grew in popularity, particularly when more and more young people left the family farm and went to the city to find work, or went to war. Agriculture changed tremendously during and after the Second World War thanks to labour shortages and the irresistible lure of manufacturing, where people could make serious money working in steel or assembling cars. America was building highways, construction was booming and jobs were plentiful. Post-war Europe underwent its own building boom, repairing and replacing all that had been destroyed during six years of war. Manufacturing took off and people all over the world left the land and went to urban areas to participate in the new era of prosperity.

According to the *Denver Post*, it was Warren Monfort, a rancher from Greeley, Colorado, who developed the idea of a 'feedlot' in 1930. Before that, most cattle were bought off the range in the autumn and transported to Chicago, Kansas City and other points on the railway to be slaughtered, processed and further distributed. Monfort recognized that if he fed his cattle on grain and forage in the winter months when grass was unavailable, he could produce a steady supply of fresh beef all year round. Soon he was providing the same service for other ranches. When his son Kenneth took over the business in the early 1950s, he further revolutionized the industry by building his own processing plant, eliminating the need for the costly and debilitating transportation of live cattle to city centres. It was this all-in-one concept of feeding and then processing animals on the same location that changed the face of the cattle business. In 1987 the company was sold for U.S.$300 million to industrial giant ConAgra.

While CAFOs were ramping up in the cattle sector, the 1970s and '80s saw pig production follow the consolidation model of poultry, moving from several hundred thousand smaller farmers to roughly 68,000 in 2015, according to the National Pork Producers Council. At the same time, production increased substantially, and while many farms are still family-owned with fewer than 5,000 pigs per farm, the farmers are not independent. Instead, they are contracted to large companies such as JBS or WH Group (the former Smithfield).

In fact, in the USA more than 75 per cent of all the pigs processed are owned by JBS USA, WH Group, Hormel or Tyson. Just four companies own the bulk of the chicken business: Tyson, Perdue, Pilgrims Pride (now owned by JBS) and Sanderson. Eighty per cent of all U.S. cattle are owned by Cargill, Tyson, JBS USA and National Beef Packing.[1]

These companies employ farmers/contractors to grow the animals in their initial stage, such as egg/chick, calf/cow or breeding/farrowing pigs. Once they are hatched or reach the requisite size, they are moved on to operations that specialize in the next stage of their grow-out. Only cattle have a life that remotely resembles what the average person thinks of as a farm animal's existence. A cow goes from the cow/calf operation to a stocker/feeder who brings them up to the ideal weight on pasture before they are sent to a feedlot for fattening on grain, typically for no more than a few months. Pigs and poultry might move from pen to pen, but they will not see the light of day, or smell fresh air. Eventually they all arrive at the processing house.

Company control extends to every facet of production. Much of the animals' feed, soy and corn, is grown by other contract farmers also employed by the company. The company, or 'integrator' as they are called, owns the milling and storage facilities as well as the slaughterhouses. This is called vertical integration. And so the era of cheap meat, at the centre of every plate and at virtually every meal, came into being.

Of course, not every country has pursued this model with the same enthusiasm as the USA, but certainly Brazil, China and even Australia are increasingly accepting the CAFO construct. Western Europe remains fairly traditional, with many smaller farms rather than the mega-agribusinesses and contract farmers that have come to dominate much of livestock production elsewhere. Perhaps because, until recently, Europeans did not aspire to major export livestock production, the CAFO remains fairly uncommon there. Nevertheless, pork and poultry are increasingly trending toward industrial production in the UK, while in Denmark and the Netherlands, the two countries that produce the bulk of Western Europe's pork supply, concentrated feeding models have definitely been adopted, though with considerable modifications to the scale of the American style.

Poultry is the fastest-growing sector in the livestock industry throughout the European Union. Top producers are Poland, France, the UK, Germany and Spain.[2] Though the European model remains more in line with traditional agriculture, allowing for family farms for example, big integrators such as Vion, Moy Park and others are well established in the EU and growing. They are contracting increasingly with farmers who are looking to expand, and who are finding it more difficult to remain independent when it comes to slaughter and processing. It is likely that the trend will continue thanks to the economies of scale made possible by vertical integration.

CAFOs could be considered a tremendous improvement over traditional animal agriculture. Putting large numbers of animals in relatively small spaces reduces the requirement for large landholdings. Producers require much less labour to keep the animals healthy. Enclosures make the tracking and control of animals easier; medications can be readily administered; if an animal is unwell, in theory, it should be easier to quarantine. Plus producers know how much food their animals are consuming. In short, it's pure genius from the point of view of profitability. Less land and less labour adds up to higher margins. Unfortunately, there is much more to this rosy picture of increased profits than the industry would have consumers know.

CAFOs can only work if the animals are really healthy. Not surprisingly, animals get sick, just as humans do. Their diseases are often highly contagious, so in a small space a disease will spread like wildfire. The sanitation in the intensive CAFO model is quite difficult to maintain, so hygiene suffers. Animals are dirty, sometimes very dirty. In worst-case scenarios, they are almost literally covered in faeces. And while that is not the norm, it is often a real challenge to maintain clean animals given the number of creatures in each space and the frequency with which they eliminate.

In order to preserve herd health, producers discovered that it was a good idea to feed all the animals a low dose of antibiotics on a daily basis to cut down on the incidence of disease. Alexander Fleming, who invented the first antibiotic in 1928, warned in the 1940s that overuse could easily breed new pathogens. The meat industry (as well as the medical community) ignored that warning. Feeding low-dose antibiotics kept herds healthy and profits high. Then another major discovery was made related to the use of the low-dose antibiotics. Animals grew faster! It was a miracle! Animals could come to market weight and be ready to ship way ahead of schedule. Cattle grew up in eighteen months instead of three years, pigs in ten months instead of eighteen to twenty, and chickens in seven weeks instead of 26! Think of how much money a producer saves in feed, water and labour when the animal can be harvested so far ahead of the normal growing period.

To this day it is not exactly known why antibiotics confer this extra bonus, but the thinking is that because the animal's immune system is not constantly working to ward off disease, the body can put all that disease-fighting energy into growth. The meat industry worldwide has grown to depend ever more heavily on the use of antibiotics as a crucial part of its strategy to grow animals at accelerated speed despite the less than ideal conditions in CAFOs. Certainly other factors go into this rapid growth, most notably nutrition, but antibiotics have made a significant contribution. This translates into unheard-of profits and explains why farmers and ranchers in the United States, Latin America and China have resisted growing calls to ban the use of low-dose antibiotics in livestock production.

Despite the fact that antibiotic-resistant pathogens began making their appearance as early as the 1950s, not many were willing to listen. By the 1970s, alarm bells were being sounded about growing resistance to common antibiotics, led by Dr Stuart Levy from Tufts University, Boston, Massachusetts, president of the International Alliance for the Prudent Use of Antibiotics. Though the United States Food and Drug Administration (FDA) attempted to step in, the powerful lobbying influence of the industry managed to block any changes to production styles. The National Antimicrobial Resistance Monitoring System, or NARMS, in the USA has categorically stated that the use of antibiotics in food-producing animals

> contributes to the emergence of antibiotic-resistant bacteria in food-producing animals. These resistant bacteria can contaminate the foods that come from those animals, and persons who consume these foods can develop antibiotic-resistant infections.[3]

Only now, since 2012, has the FDA published a series of 'guidances' for the U.S. meat industry to ratchet down use of antibiotics important to human medicine in livestock feed for the purpose of 'growth promotion'. By 2017 the use of antibiotics in livestock production in the USA will be controlled by veterinarians rather than farmers and ranchers. How compliance will be monitored and enforced is a question that has not yet been fully answered.

Western Europe, which has adopted many of the U.S. methods of livestock production, though by no means at the same scale, has been far more circumspect in its use of these drugs. While antibiotics remain in use there, the quantities involved are not even close to what is pumped into U.S. livestock. Some countries are more advanced in their phase-out of the routine use of antibiotics, with northern Europe being the leader, while countries in the southern and eastern sectors seem less interested.

The Danes were the first to recognize that multi-drug-resistant pathogens were already a problem within their animal populations, and increasingly a threat to humans. In 1999 the Danish government imposed a ban on using antibiotics as growth promoters, and tightened controls so that only a veterinarian can write a prescription for the drugs. At first they lost a lot of pigs (clearly delighting the Americans, who pointed to this initial mortality as proof that withdrawing those antibiotics would have disastrous consequences for the health of the animals), but the Danes soon learned to manage their pigs more successfully, with improved vaccines and probiotics, as well as better hygiene. The Danish Experiment, as it came to be known, proved that depriving herds of low-dose antibiotics does *not* in fact result in the losses feared by other pork-producing nations. Several years later the Netherlands, another major EU producer of pork, followed suit with similar success, reducing its use of antibiotics by as much as 60 per cent.[4] Today, thanks to the EU protocols governing the use of antibiotics and other drugs in livestock production, no farmer has access to antibiotics without a prescription and oversight from a licensed veterinarian. Coincidentally the incidence of multi-drug-resistant pathogens has also declined.

The danger of using antibiotics as profligately as we have done cannot be overstated. Dr Margaret Chan of the World Health Organization (WHO) said this in a recent speech:

> The rise of antimicrobial resistance is a global health crisis. Medicine is losing more and more mainstay antimicrobials as pathogens develop resistance. Second-line treatments are less effective, more costly, more toxic, and sometimes extremely difficult to administer. Many are also in short supply . . . With few replacement products in the pipeline, the world

> is heading towards a post-antibiotic era in which common infections will once again kill.[5]

Numerous organizations have issued similar warnings, including the British Ministry of Health, the Food and Agriculture Organization of the United Nations (FAO) and the Centers for Disease Control. Why is overuse of antibiotics so dangerous? According to Urvashi Rangan, who directs the Consumer Safety and Sustainability Group for Consumer Reports,

> Studies have shown that regardless of what kind of antibiotic is being used, whether important to human health such as the cephalosporins, penicillins and others, or not, such as ionophores, the bacteria do not differentiate. They eventually develop resistances to all drugs, within any class.[6]

Once that happens, they become nearly indestructible. New strains of common bacteria such as *Salmonella*, *E. coli* and *Campylobacter* have become what is known as multi-drug-resistant, making those diseases increasingly difficult to treat even with combinations of several antibiotics.

It should be noted that one of the most common misperceptions about the use of antibiotics in the food chain is that the antibiotics are still in the meat when we eat it. That is not the case. All food animals, no matter where they are from, are expected to undergo a mandatory withdrawal process of several days' or weeks' duration from their prophylactic antibiotics. There may be trace residue still, but that is presumably monitored by food safety protocols and is not the primary danger to consumers, contrary to popular belief. The most specific danger lies in the multi-drug-resistant pathogens that have survived the antibiotics and are now able to thrive in spite of them. *Salmonella*, *E. coli* and *Campylobacter* are pathogens that exist on the surface of all meat to some degree, no matter how organic, natural and fresh it may be. In the new drug-resistant versions of these common diseases, the symptoms are far more virulent and difficult to treat. The existence of these pathogens on the surface of meat, or inside it when it is ground or 'needle tenderized', is what constitutes the danger to consumers. Industrially produced meat has been shown to carry a very high pathogen load. This increases the risk that significant illness or even fatalities can result (particularly among the very young, the elderly or the immune-compromised) if there is a failure to follow stringent food safety measures in the home or restaurant kitchen.

The Chinese, bedevilled by food safety issues, are in the process of converting their meat production from the traditional smallholder to the CAFOs for which the Americans are famous. In 2013 they purchased Smithfield, the largest producer of pork in the United States, not only for its pork production, but for the highly developed biosecurity measures that help to create a safe food supply. For the same reason, they have invited the Tyson Foods giant in to help them with their poultry production. Chinese use of antibiotics in the CAFO context dwarfs even that of the United States. Recently, strains of bacteria resistant to the 'last resort' antibiotic, Colistin, were discovered, to the great consternation of many public health organizations including the WHO.

Nevertheless, China continues to deploy and to sell to its farmers vast quantities of antibiotics deemed to be 'important in human medicine', including the cephalosporins (now banned from animal production in the USA) as well as tetracycline and penicillin-based drugs. China produces half of the world's pork supply,[7] and is the second largest poultry producer in the world.[8] Animals and humans can and do trade bacteria readily. Normally these transfers are benign, but in the case of certain bacteria, the swapping of microbes can result in serious illnesses, such as MRSA (methicillin-resistant *Staphylococcus aureus*). Farm and slaughterhouse workers have been found to be colonized with some of the same multi-drug-resistant gut microbes, and then into the greater community at large.

With the close physical association between many farmers and animals, there have been a multitude of cases of multi-drug-resistant disease. The government is finally beginning to pay attention to the dangers in feeding not just animals, but humans, too many antibiotics.[9] Currently their use is estimated as being as high as 75 million pounds (34 million kg) per year in livestock production alone, including drugs essential to human medicine.[10]

Brazil is also culpable for excessive use of antibiotics in its animal production. The use of prophylactic antibiotics to enhance growth and prevent disease is what allows the CAFO to be so profitable and successful, particularly in countries where facility hygiene is less well established, and protocols lax, if they exist at all. Bear in mind that Brazil's mega-agribusiness, JBS, operates in 24 countries on five continents. It is the world's largest producer of meat products, including pork, poultry, beef and lamb. At the 2016 International Processing and Production Exposition, one Brazilian pharmaceutical salesman guiltily conceded that Brazil has few regulations on the use of antibiotics, or indeed any other drugs typical to animal production. And while the EU and other countries have strict limits on drug residues or even the types of drugs or hormones used in raising livestock, many other customer nations do not. For example, Brazil sells much of its beef to the Middle East, Asia and smaller countries elsewhere. In any case, most of the protocols surrounding imports and exports have to do with veterinary certifications on animal health or welfare, disease control and other factors. Typically the major concerns surround issues such as the presence of highly contagious diseases such as foot-and-mouth or avian flu.

India has perhaps the worst problem with antibiotics, according to a 2015 study from Princeton University. With the extraordinary number of diseases prevalent in the local population, the excessive use of antibiotics in India has already caused them serious problems with antibiotic-resistant bacteria. Despite all the information that has become available on the subject in the last decade, neither the healthcare nor the livestock industry appear to be making the necessary adjustments to how these precious drugs are used. They are overprescribed in both categories, and estimates suggest that industrial use at least will more than double by 2030, leaving the world's population vulnerable to diseases thought to be erased long ago.[11] This is a matter of the utmost seriousness to public health, and world leaders need to take the necessary steps to educate industry and humans alike in the very real possibility that we may soon find ourselves living in a post-antibiotic world.

CAFOs are growing fastest in developing countries anxious to participate in what they believe is the economic salvation of producing cheap meat at higher profit margins. Part of this growth is due to international companies such as Cargill, Tyson and JBS building facilities around the world to capitalize on the increasing appetite for meat that comes as a corollary to higher living standards and per capita incomes. China, Brazil and India are not the only countries to embrace either the idea behind intensive production, or the companies that are so good at using that model. Throughout Southeast Asia, industrialized meat production is growing swiftly. What's more, in countries where food safety protocols are problematic, the know-how of a Tyson or a Cargill is an added incentive. These companies provide valuable training in biosecurity for developing countries, especially those where a great deal of the livestock is still in the hands of small farms, such as in Vietnam. Wet markets, where animals are slaughtered or cut up on demand, are more common in those countries. And given the high probability of disease where raw meat is left unrefrigerated and often covered in flies or other insects, a Western-style model of cleanliness can provide an emerging country's government with some much-needed protections for its population. The downside is that the combination of heavy antibiotic use and tight confinement has given rise to many of the same multi-drug-resistant pathogens seen in Western countries. In other words, while the benefits of scale and efficiency have been championed, none of the more dangerous aspects of the CAFO model seem to have been communicated as urgently.

Indeed, evidence compiled by entities such as the FAO, numerous universities, advocacy groups and independent research has shown the widespread damage that the CAFO model inflicts on animals, workers, the environment and rural communities. Yet the meat industry continually promotes the CAFO as the only possible way to provide adequate nutrition and satisfy consumer demands with the least input and lowest carbon footprint.

While all those savings exist, they do so only because so many of the actual costs are not reflected in the day-to-day operations of a CAFO. Soil degradation from planting the same feed crops over and over, with inadequate fallowing or rotation, along with extensive water and air pollution, is typically ignored by the industry, and the surrounding populations bear the consequences. Those issues are just the tip of the iceberg of major problems with the CAFO model, but farmers all over the world have bought into it largely because the industry is so consolidated that they have few other competitive choices for how they can process and distribute the meat from their animals.

As we will see in subsequent chapters, the trend of 'vertical integration' and industry consolidation has forced farmers to adopt methods that they may personally find abhorrent but accept due to limited options. In spite of growing evidence that a more agro-ecological approach to farming, with a mix of feed and food crops along with animals, is far better for the future of our food supply, the CAFO continues to expand its reach across borders and into rural communities.[12]

2
THE BUSINESS OF GENETICS

Every country that produces livestock has developed its own special breeds over the course of millennia. There may be dozens of breeds for each species, a reflection of the highly diversified farming that went on in previous centuries. Those breeds came about from farmers carefully observing and cross-breeding their animals with those of other farmers, and developing animals that were acutely suited to their environment and food opportunities. Some of the breeds were exported to the New World and crossed with animals indigenous to those areas. Cross-breeding confers 'hybrid vigour', also called 'heterosis'. Achieving hybrid vigour means selecting for traits that enhance a breed, pairing up genetic material that doesn't overlap or dominate all other traits.

Hybrid vigour is essential to keeping animals healthy and productive. Cross-breeding is hugely important to agriculture, and is an art as well as a science. Not only are farmers selecting animals on the basis of yield, reproduction and growth, but they are gambling on including less obvious traits such as good mothering, docility and the all-important consideration of flavour. That is where the art of breeding really shows. Agricultural fairs around the world show the most refined examples of the art as an advertisement for best practices, as well as providing a place for livestock farmers to trade genes.

Independent farmers use the equivalent of the county fair to make the transactions that will most enhance their breeding stock. Some farmers augment their farm income by selling semen to other farmers for artificial insemination. They might tout their females as great breeders. Most independent livestock farmers keep very extensive records called 'breeder books' that can trace the lineage of a herd or flock back for generations. Breed associations catalogue and archive this information so that traits that disappear or reappear can be traced back to their origins and bred either in or out as necessary. Cross-breeding can take multiple generations to achieve the desired result, and breeder books are invaluable in keeping track of the development of a particular strain in livestock. Nearly every 'heritage', or old-fashioned, breed has an association. Producers who specialize in a particular breed often become members to find other like-minded farmers with whom they can buy, swap or breed new stock.

In the CAFO model, animals have been hybridized to withstand the pressures of growing out in close confinement, on a particular diet and in a very short time frame. Not many breeds can thrive in the conditions presented by a CAFO, so industrialized meat production has pumped billions of dollars into breeding ones that can. As a result, most pigs, cattle and poultry are derived from a very short list of genetic packages.[1]

The way it works is that genetics companies, of which there are a handful that represent each category – whether bovine, ovine, poultry or swine – test, test and retest different combinations of bird or beast until they find one that has the best chance for success within the industrial model. These scientists can breed for increased milk production, bigger litters, hard shells, big yolks, certain immunities and a host of other refinements that will yield the maximum profit. Obviously they breed for size, texture, more or less fat, conformation or shape, colour and so forth. But who would ever have thought that actual character traits such as aggression or docility could be part of genetic selection? And yet it is so. For example, as the world moves away from the stackable connected battery cages used to house laying hens, geneticists are trying to figure out how to keep hens from pecking each other when they are allowed to move around more easily in an 'enriched' cage that gives the birds a little more room and maybe a perch, or are grown in an open aviary system.

Genetics companies provide 'pure' strains of the ideal animal. To do this they use four lines: cross a male and a female, then cross those offspring with the offspring of another male/female pair. This gives hybrid vigour. They do maintain a gene pool of many lines, including heritage breeds, and other experimental lines they have preserved. But as the companies have developed the science, the pool of genetics seems to have become more consolidated as they get closer to the 'ideal' bird. As the market changes, the geneticists are able to re-tool the package, and they do. Then the company sells the resulting hybridization package as the purest expression of the animal that best fits industrial needs. Some producers work with 'grandparents', some with 'parents', but all the animals that follow possess the genes of that 'pure' expression. The offspring from those select packages are sold in their millions to growers around the world. There will be some differences according to geography that will be bred into the 'pure' strains: for countries having hotter or colder weather, different food, varying fat requirements and size preferences. All of these features are isolated and bred either in or out, but the bottom line is that animals destined for the industrial market represent a comparatively small pool from which literally billions of animals are grown.

In the poultry industry, for example, just four companies supply the majority of the genetics worldwide: Aviagen in the USA, Wesjohann Group in Germany, Hendrix-Genetics in the Netherlands and Cobb-Vantress (a wholly owned subsidiary of Tyson Foods).[2] In recent years some of those companies have developed joint development agreements, teaming up to share expertise on breeding the perfect chicken. Those same genetics are sold from the USA to India, from the UK to China. Cobb-Vantress operates in more than 90 countries and Hendrix in 24, with consultations in 100. These companies sell the majority of all the poultry in the world, both laying hens and broilers, in some cases along with other livestock species. In the USA alone, poultry production tops nine million broilers per year. The industry pooh-poohs the idea that this lack of genetic diversity could potentially lead to disaster if a disease emerged to which there was no resistance.

Consider the amazing development of the Cornish Cross. This chicken literally transformed the poultry industry by achieving market weight in 45 days. The typical old-fashioned chicken takes at least six months to arrive at that same weight. In the 1930s the Cornish Cross resulted from breeding the

Cornish breed, which boasts heavy breast meat, with White Rock chickens. Though still called the Cornish Cross, over the intervening years the birds sold in supermarkets have been even more heavily selected than the original, focusing on rapid growth and enormous breasts. The result is the broilers we have come to assume are the natural descendants of the junglefowl or *Gallus gallus*, the ancestor of domestic chickens, but they are very different in looks. There are significant animal welfare consequences to this particular genetic package, but the profitability for industry is indisputable.

Genetic manipulation can also help animals give birth to more babies. Recently a *New York Times* article by the American investigative reporter Michael Moss rocked the agricultural world by describing reproduction and various other breeding experiments being conducted at the U.S. Meat Animal Research Center in Clay Center, Nebraska. He described efforts to increase litter size in pigs from eight to fourteen and the impact on the sow, and especially the piglets, many frail and underweight from so much crowding in the womb. Meanwhile the sow has been bred to be much larger to accommodate such a big litter, resulting in more infant mortality as her bulk crushes to death the babies too weak to move out of the way.[3] The article was deplored by the Center as well as the industry for being unfair and inaccurate, but the source of the article was Dr James Keen, a veterinarian who had been employed by the Center for over a decade. He was alarmed by what he felt were egregious animal welfare issues being raised by the experimentation. At his request, the *New York Times* launched an investigation.

Though the animal agricultural industry and the Center cried foul, ultimately they were forced by further internal investigations to improve their performance in a multitude of ways.

Bigger animals, faster-growing, heat-tolerant, more babies . . . you name it, the 'good' traits have been selected and introduced to breeding stock. However, genetic selection always implies a trade-off of characteristics. So though a bigger breast or more babies may result from cross-breeding, it's easily possible that disease resistance, or tractability, will be bred out. Many of these 'improved' breeds suffer from skeletal malformations, a result of tinkering with genes, and compromised immune systems. In order to combat the dangers presented by having so many animals from the same gene pool, genetics companies consider the other major part of their job is promoting 'biosecurity' for their embryos, semen, eggs and babies. For example, if a genetic scientist has visited a farm, biosecurity dictates that it will be 72 hours before they can return to a lab, so as not to bring in any unwanted pathogens. Maintaining viable stocks of genes in multiple locations is another facet of maintaining biosecurity. In addition, all animal facilities, whether research centres, intensive production facilities or labs, practise rigorous biosecurity measures. If a disease enters a chicken or pig house, every animal in it can and probably will become infected. The pathogens will be in the bedding, litter and air system and on every surface. Given the less than robust health of confined animals, the unfortunate by-product of the breeding programme, any breach of their biosecurity is a potential for financial disaster. The genetics companies provide extensive and near-constant training in how to keep animals safe in their houses, and far away from people not properly showered or garbed.

We don't yet have genetically modified animals in the food system but it will undoubtedly happen. Research into inserting genes from one animal breed to another is ongoing, while other techniques include 'gene editing'. One firm in Korea has successfully bred a pig with enormous back legs, or hams, thanks to the editing of the gene that governs muscle growth. By looking at the genes in Belgian Blues, a cattle breed with massive muscular hindquarters, scientists discovered how to arrive at the same result in pigs, but without the long process of cross-breeding and selection that created the Belgian Blue. Other gene-editing techniques could produce non-allergenic milk, or hornless cattle.[4] Most recently, production of a genetically modified chicken was greenlighted by the FDA because the egg whites contain a valuable enzyme to treat a rare disease, lysosomal acid lipase deficiency. Neither chicken nor egg will be released into the food supply.[5] Instead they will be funnelled right into pharmacology. Rabbits and goats have also been genetically modified to produce certain products valuable to pharmacology.[6]

The Chinese have announced plans to invest heavily in cloning technology and declared that they will raise a million cloned cattle a year to meet the increasing demand for beef in Asia. The cloning facility will be the largest in the world to date and will include a gene bank.[7] It remains to be seen how their public will react to consuming cloned meat, as up until now it has received a resounding thumbs-down, at least from Western consumers. Cultural differences may enable the Chinese to sell their cloned beef successfully in their own country or to some of their trading partners.

Scientists have already successfully cloned cattle and sheep – remember Dolly? In 1996 Dolly was the first animal cloned from an adult cell. Since then researchers have assiduously worked to find a way to successfully clone livestock. Cloning can provide a very valuable resource in the way of preserving successful genes in livestock that might otherwise die out if only one or two animals have a particular natural immunity or trait. For example, cloning helped to save a gene in one bull that was found to be resistant to the very common cattle disease brucellosis. No other bull was found to have that natural immunity, so his clone is preserved in a gene bank awaiting the moment when large-scale cloning becomes commonplace. In any case, unless the Chinese have had a major breakthrough in cloning technology unknown to the rest of the world, they will have an uphill battle. Cloning rarely results in a live birth, and if the animal survives birth it typically dies in just a few days. Though, in theory, cloning should result in a replica, more often than not there are major abnormalities in vascular development, along with all kinds of problems with size and function of the heart, liver and lungs. In addition, cloning seems to express itself in making abnormally large babies, or occasionally dwarfism. Still it's not hard to imagine a future where cloned livestock is conventional rather than extraordinary in the food chain.[8]

Though cloning and genetically modified animals may become commonplace, the most valuable resource in preserving the best in livestock remains the precious heritage breeds. These animals are typically the quintessential expression of the particular region from where they originate. They have qualities that current livestock production will often discard in favour of faster growth, more rapid conversion of feed to muscle, specific conformations and the like. Heritage breeds tend to be far more flavourful, a quality that should be but isn't always to everyone's taste. They have smaller litters if they are pigs, less milk if they are dairy cattle, and are smaller in size if they are beef cattle. They are much slower to come to market weight and cost commensurately more in food, water and labour than the industrialized breeds currently in production. For the obvious economic reasons these unique breeds fell out of favour with large-scale livestock producers. The amazing advances that animal sciences have made with their understanding of genomic sequencing, feed directives and the use of growth promotants have rendered the heritage breed obsolete in the context of the global meat supply.

However, heritage breeds are the repository of genes that could easily go extinct if the breed dies out. They can play a critical role in the overall biodiversity of any environment. They are participants in an ecosystem where every part is necessary to maintain the whole. They may provide unique ingredients to soil and plant health through their excrement. Their foraging may eliminate weeds or invasive plant species. Heritage breeds are typically far more robust in health and more resistant to disease than their industrialized brethren.

In Newport, Rhode Island, a special kind of bank has been established. It is called the SVF Foundation. Established in 1999, the SVF (or Swiss Village Farm) has dedicated itself to preserving the germplasm (that is, tissue) of heritage breeds before they become extinct. The foundation collects and cryogenically conserves semen and embryos of each livestock breed that still exists. The purpose is to protect our global food supply by preserving the unique breeds that have developed around the world, each with its own special traits. With the preservation of the genetics, any one of these breeds could be revived within a generation, offering a defence against a replay of the nineteenth-century Irish Potato Famine. You might wonder why there is an analogy between potatoes and animals. Peculiar as that may sound, it is actually very apt. The reason is that industrialized farming, whether plant or animal, tends to concentrate very heavily on one particular cultivar, in the case of plants, or breed, in the case of animals. Recently headlines have been made about how the banana as we know it may well become a thing of the past. Why? Because banana plantations have reduced the variety of their plants down to one main cultivar, which is at this moment being ravaged by a disease particular to that plant. Production of the 'Cavendish', the most popular banana, has virtually ceased as horticulturalists seek for ways to revive the breed either through soil management, or through hybridization with a strain of the plant that confers resistance to that disease. The same reasoning will apply to animals bred for confinement.

As we slowly discover the roles of species in the overall health of the environment as well as their essential place in an integrated farming programme, the need to revive and conserve these disappearing breeds becomes ever more apparent. Even some of the genetics companies, such as the Dutch giant Hendrix, are developing their own repositories of heritage genetics. Recognizing the value of the older breeds for disease resistance and overall robustness, more and more farmers in Europe are looking to raise those animals rather than the industrial favourites. Many more consumers are enjoying the superiority of heritage breeds from a gastronomic standpoint, and this too is fuelling a renaissance of sorts. Worldwide, heritage livestock breed conservancies, devoted to identifying local and regional strains and encouraging their production, are multiplying. The animals these organizations foster will never fit into the mould of the industrial production methods, but they may well come to the rescue when factory-farmed animals succumb to disease disaster.

3
LIVESTOCK AND DISEASE

All animals carry disease, or bacteria that can cause disease. Many are specific to one species while others can move freely between them. This chapter will discuss the most common diseases that affect livestock agriculture and human beings. There are literally hundreds of diseases that can make the leap between humans and animals, but in the main they are limited to geographic regions or particular cultures. Eating 'bushmeat' in Africa, for example, passes dozens of these pathogens or 'zoonoses' from animal to human and sickens thousands of people annually. In developed countries where food systems are more reliable, that number comes down to just a handful.

Probably no single disease has had a greater impact on people in the developed world than has the devastating epidemic of bovine spongiform encephalopathy (BSE), dubbed 'mad cow disease' by the tabloids. This ghastly episode terrorized the beef-eating public and decimated the cattle industry of the UK for over a decade.

In 1986 a number of cattle in the UK were reported as inexplicably losing weight, falling down, becoming aggressive or demonstrating other peculiar behaviours before dropping dead. Farmers and veterinarians had never seen anything like it. Post-mortem studies revealed that the brains of affected animals showed areas of spongy tissue riddled with holes, often in a daisy-like pattern. At the time it was thought to be a form of scrapie, a similar and well-known disease that affects sheep, and part of a group of diseases known as transmissible spongiform encephalopathies. Scrapie, however, does not jump the species barrier, and this new bovine form was a complete mystery. Over a period of ten years, the epidemic killed 170,000 cows, and resulted in the slaughter of over four million more in an effort to eradicate the disease.[1]

Once the details of this obscure new disease went public, British beef exports were banned in the EU. Domestic beef consumption fell to an all-time low as the epidemic gained strength and more animals were affected. Farmers were given some compensation for the loss of their cattle, but the impact on agriculture and ancillary businesses was devastating, and cost British taxpayers billions. The epidemic peaked in 1992 and 1993. Eventually it was discovered – or rather theorized, as the disease is still poorly understood – that cattle fed animal protein that contained tissues from bovine brains and spinal cords contracted the disease. This led to a series of profound changes in slaughtering, rendering and feeding cattle, along with modifications to how humans can donate blood and how that blood is processed. Particularly in the UK and Western Europe, blood donors were screened for possible exposure to VCJD through their diet. Because of the long incubation period, any blood donation was tested for the disease, lest it enter the population through blood transfusions.

Though the incidence of BSE in cattle diminished, in 1995 a young man of 21, Stephen Churchill, was diagnosed with a variant of Creutzfeldt–Jakob disease, a deadly degenerative neurological disease of considerable rarity. Unlike its original namesake, this strain, dubbed VCJD (variant Creutzfeldt–Jakob disease), attacked much younger people than the norm, and took quite a bit longer to kill the victim. It also incubated more quickly. Typical CJD can take up to thirty years to manifest in a human. In these British cases it was a matter of a few years. What the victims had in common was the consumption of hamburger patties made from British beef. In the next four years another 176 victims would die in the UK and Ireland, with roughly fifty more cases appearing in other countries.

The epidemic and the subsequent human tragedies were exacerbated by foot-dragging on the part of the UK Ministry of Agriculture, Fisheries and Food in comprehending and managing the risks, not to mention informing the public. Understandably the ministry was anxious to protect the British cattle industry, so quite a bit of relevant information was suppressed in the early part of the epidemic. Eventually the oversight of the food supply in Britain was given over to a newly created agency, the Food Standards Agency. Though BSE is almost eradicated now, thanks to the feeding ban on bovine spinal cord tissue and brains, the disease is known to persist in a cow's body for at least eight years. To prevent further outbreaks, a ban on the slaughter of cows over thirty months of age was imposed in 1996. Cattle younger than thirty months do not seem to develop the disease. By 2005 a test had been developed that can identify older cattle with the disease, and the thirty-month ban had been rescinded in the UK.[2]

Why the UK suffered so much from BSE, when other major cattle-producing countries did not, most likely stems from the reliance on animal proteins as feed for cattle. All the bits of the animal that don't go into food production for pets or people are 'rendered' into highly nutritious meat, blood and bonemeal. The poultry industry contributes similarly, with feather meal and 'poultry litter' (really gross and just what you think it is) being a significant additive to feed as well. With relatively little grassland on which to graze cattle, UK farmers rely quite heavily on animal protein as a key component for nourishing their livestock. The USA, Australia and South America all have ample grazing, and typically cattle there receive far less animal protein in their feed. With the UK as an example of how not to manage a livestock epidemic, other countries, and especially the USA, have aggressively enacted BSE controls. International protocols on feed directives and other measures to protect cattle and people are still evolving. To this day the UK still suffers reputationally from the fact that BSE undermined public confidence in agriculture and the agencies meant to protect consumer health.[3]

Beyond BSE there are the very real dangers of influenza, whether avian (bird) flu or swine flu. The flu virus is a particularly tricky customer no matter its origins. A swiftly evolving organism, influenza can jump from species to species, travelling on the wind until it finds a likely host and settles in to wreak havoc. Bird and swine flu are simply variants of the basic virus, though they both tend to be more virulent than the common flu. Thanks to their ferocity they are considered fearsome opponents by public health organizations, who watch their progress closely as they move from country to country.

There have been multiple outbreaks of the H1N1 swine flu, but none so devastating as the pandemic of 2009 when some 74 countries worldwide reported infections in the human population. Genotyping of the virus showed it to be a mix of multiple strains, including avian flu viruses from North America along with swine flu viruses from North America, Europe and Asia, mixed in with strains typical of human disease.[4] The mixing of the viral strains was evidently the reason it spread so quickly through the human population. The CDC, or Center for Disease Control in the USA, reported in 2012 that the mortality figures worldwide were somewhere between 151,700 and 575,400, a huge range admittedly.[5] Given that the hardest-hit areas were Southeast Asia and Africa, accurate numbers are hard to come by. Moreover, many people perished from ancillary infections such as viral pneumonia, a frequent co-pathogen with the flu. Countries around the world have cooperated in developing vaccines, along with preparedness models, in order to stem another outbreak of this magnitude. Still, with the rapidity with which the influenza virus evolves, it is clear that we are fortunate that a worse scenario has not yet emerged, given the global nature of traffic in humans and animals.

Far more common, though not to humans, are avian influenzas (AI) or bird flus. Incidents of humans contracting this disease have been mostly confined to Asia, where nearly all the AI strains dwell. Bird flu is thought to have originated in Asia, a by-product of its open-air poultry markets. The strain that has evolved in recent years is called Highly Pathogenic Avian Influenza A or HPAI H5N1. Since 2003 the disease has infected six hundred people in fifteen countries. While largely sparing human populations, enormous outbreaks of AI have occurred in the last few years, resulting in epic numbers of poultry being slaughtered and disposed of. In 2014–15 in the United States alone nearly fifty million birds either died or were slaughtered to prevent further spread of the disease. The Chinese poultry industry lost U.S.$6.5 billion in 2013.[6] Europe had its share of cases in 2015, mostly in France, as well as the UK, the Netherlands, Bulgaria and Hungary. All of the countries affected in the EU member states have cooperated in a rigorous policy of biosecurity implemented in a coordinated fashion. The situation remains closely monitored and no cases of human infection have been reported. Nonetheless, due to the high mutability of avian influenza, most infectious disease centres note a distinct possibility of a further evolution in the virus that could make human transmission easier, resulting in the kind of pandemic that strikes terror.

How does avian influenza spread? The short answer is through migratory patterns of wild birds. Where they flock, nest or just rest, they shed the virus through their droppings. Typically the virus does not affect wild birds, but infected domesticated poultry such as chickens or turkeys literally drop like flies. Some theories suggest that poultry flocks from concentrated feeding operations are particularly vulnerable, whereas backyard flocks have more immunity. Given the limited scope of the gene pool from which industrial poultry is selected, that theory may have some credibility, but it is by no means confirmed.

Infinitely more common diseases that migrate from animal to human are what most people think of as 'food poisoning'. Common food-borne illnesses can be laid at the door of bacteria in the gut of all animals, including humans. In a groundbreaking 2015 report on food-borne illnesses published by the WHO, the number of people said to be affected globally by these all-too-common diseases truly beggars belief.[7] While the report identified 31 common diseases spread through food, the most ubiquitous are salmonellosis, *E. coli*, listeriosis and campylobacteriosis. Around the world the WHO estimates that one in ten, or roughly 600 million, people will be infected by some form of food-borne illness yearly, and nearly half a million of them will die as a result.[8] The prevalence of these illnesses disproportionately affects children under five years old. Not surprisingly, poorer countries have the highest incidence of disease, but developed countries, with presumably the technology and education to prevent thousands of cases, rack up big numbers as well. The WHO report is meant to provide tools for governments to develop strategies in hygiene, education and training to help bring those numbers down.

Just five pathogens, non-typhoidal *Salmonella*, *Campylobacter*, *Listeria*, *E. coli* and norovirus, make more than 220 million people ill every year worldwide. However, unlike *E. coli*, salmonellosis, listeriosis and campylobacteriosis, norovirus is a true virus and is not acquired from eating food. Instead, norovirus is spread directly from person to person through contact with surfaces and even clothing, or by sharing food or drink, and is highly infectious. The bacterial diseases are caused only by food and cannot be acquired through contact with an infected person. In any case, all of these diseases are highly preventable simply by deploying stringent hygiene in animal housing and production and safe food handling.

The four bacterial agents can also cause permanent damage in a dizzying variety of infernal complications – most notably kidney damage, but occasionally reactive arthritis and irritable bowel syndrome. They can also create a local infection in other parts of the body. In the worst cases, the initial infections can cause death, generally through acute dehydration. The loss of productivity, the cost of treating the disease and the long-term impacts of falling ill are practically incalculable. Were an invading army to kill a quarter of a million citizens and create this much havoc and economic loss, any government would spare no expense to defend its citizens. Somehow when the enemy is microscopic, it does not excite the same bloodlust despite the devastating human impact.

Food-borne illness is acquired through poor personal hygiene, unsafe handling practices, water pollution or the consumption of undercooked meat, raw milk, juice, dairy, fruits and vegetables. Because *Salmonella*, *Campylobacter*, *Listeria* and *E. coli* bacteria are prevalent in every part of the globe, and most often associated with meat consumption, it is best to focus here on their stories.

E. coli, or *Escherichia coli*, contamination is one of the most common sources of diarrhoeal food-borne illness. A report from the National Center for Biotechnology Information in the USA proposes that every year nearly three million cases of acute illness worldwide are derived from a particularly virulent strain of the bacteria known as Shiga toxin-producing *Escherichia coli*. Some 3,000–4,000 of those affected will go on to develop kidney failure, hemolytic uremic syndrome or HUS, which can require dialysis treatment for weeks if not months or years. In some cases, especially among the elderly, the very young and the immune-compromised, this disease can be fatal.[9]

The strain of *E. coli* most associated with mortality and HUS is the strain that eventually came to be labelled O157:H7. *E. coli* has many different types, most of which are harmless to man and animals. While all *E. coli* organisms are ever-evolving, some critics of the meat industry suggest there are reasons why O157:H7 is so deadly. One explanation is the incidence of acidification in the rumen of the cow, caused by eating grain instead of grass. This causes the *E. coli* to evolve to be resistant to acid and explains why human stomach acid will typically stop *E. coli*, but not this variety. In addition, O157:H7 is more often found in the gut of an animal raised on antibiotics.

What changed everything about food safety in the USA was a major food-borne illness outbreak in 1993. The incident occurred in a West Coast fast-food chain called Jack in the Box. A total of 693 people were ultimately diagnosed with O157:H7, and four children died.[10] So many people were ill all at once that it became a huge news story and people across the country were outraged and frightened. The company was successfully sued individually and in a class action suit. In court documents it was revealed that the company knew that it was supposed to cook its hamburgers to 68.3°C internally, enough to kill the bacteria. Unfortunately they felt that made their burgers too tough, so they deliberately undercooked them.[11] Ultimately the restaurant chain paid out over U.S.$50 million in settlements to victims and their families.

The Jack in the Box outbreak was very instructional. The case generated a massive shift in focus towards improved food safety in both government and industry. After much pushback from the meat industry, in 2011, 0157:H7 and six of its Shiga toxin-producing cousins were labelled as 'adulterants'. Now any meat testing positive for one of these bacteria is withdrawn from production and cannot be sold. This measure and other new protocols in hygiene and testing have certainly reduced the number of reported cases of *E. coli*-related food poisoning in the United States. Nonetheless, Shiga toxin-producing *E. coli* remains a culprit in transmitting disease, though it may not be found as often in meat. As a strategy for waste management in CAFOs, livestock manure is used as agricultural fertilizer. *E. coli* has been implicated in outbreaks that stem from vegetables, fruits, alfalfa sprouts, unpasteurized milk, juice or ciders, and of course from the hands of contaminated workers in agriculture or food service.

Meat production at any stage is a dirty business. Bacteria will hitch a ride on just about anything that moves, including dust. So it is reasonable to expect that any system, no matter how nearly perfect, will have a few gaps where pathogenic bacteria get through the process intact. Thanks to their increasing antibiotic resistance, those pathogens may also be hugely pumped up to withstand any remedy save for rest and fluids. In developing nations where a cold chain (refrigeration/refrigerated transportation) is not well established, or meat is slaughtered and distributed in a 'wet market', a high load of bacteria is unavoidable. However, in industrialized nations such as the USA where the systems are sophisticated, consumers have to wonder why food-borne illness, along with massive recalls of meat due to contamination, is so commonplace as to be ignored by media and consumers alike. They shouldn't be. The related costs in loss of productivity, lost income and medical care are estimated at $15.6 billion every year in the USA alone.[12]

In a hog or poultry house, or a feedlot with 10,000 cattle, pigs or chickens, dust from hay or feed, dirt and excrement combine to create a bacteria cloud that covers every animal. The degree of filth will depend on the financial investments in equipment and labour, and the personal expertise in livestock production of the individual operator. Once at market weight the animals go to the processor. Transportation from a feedlot or other facility can take as long as 24 hours, during which time the animals are crowded together and sanitation procedures are well-nigh impossible. Upon arrival at the processing plant, where conditions remain quite confined, the animals can be coated with faeces from their journey. Washing them before slaughter would be too expensive in energy and water, and additionally stress the animals. Other measures are employed post-slaughter instead.

Among those interventions are highly engineered facilities: precision techniques for cutting; ultraviolet light bacterial detection; bleach and vinegar rinsing; and a host of other sexy inventions designed to eliminate a sick-inducing pathogen load. This is a rather curious conundrum. With all the money and know-how invested in state-of-the-art plants that big corporations pay for, it is hard to understand why there is a single molecule left of *E. coli*, *Campylobacter* or anything else for that matter. But there is.

Indeed, animal slaughter has achieved remarkable efficiency in its most advanced, industrialized form. The process is a miracle of thoughtful engineering, from the stunning box to the last chop. Every step might employ a strategy to counter inadvertent contamination, such as an antimicrobial rinse after skinning or de-feathering, or dipping a knife in a sanitizer every time the blade is sharpened. There is an obvious self-interest for any producer in maintaining a healthy food supply. The cost of being implicated in sickness is calculated in share price. Meat is a commodity on the stock market. Loss of consumer confidence in a brand can be a multimillion-dollar catastrophe. Yet despite these sophisticated interventions, food-borne illness remains rampant even in highly evolved production scenarios. So one really must ask the question, why are people still getting sick from eating meat that comes from industry sources? The answer is not obvious, but there are undoubtedly industry practices that can and should be addressed in order to reduce the incidence of illnesses. For example, one can point to the incredible speed that is typical when cutting up carcasses as one possible source of contamination. People make mistakes, especially when taxed with processing hundreds if not thousands of animals per hour. Another factor could be the relatively small number of inspectors on a production line due to budget cuts, as well as industry insistence that it should police itself instead of submitting to regulatory agencies. Those two particular issues are totally ignored or hotly disputed by the industry when confronted by a food-borne illness outbreak, or the need for a large recall due to the discovery of contamination.

Ground (minced) and tenderized meat are easily the main culprits in spreading infection from any of these food-borne bacteria. Because of the nooks and crannies in ground meat, or the thousands of tiny holes in needle-tenderized meat, bacteria are introduced from the surface to the interior. Additionally, ground meat is often a product of animals aggregated from multiple sources and even countries, which introduces a whole new level of food safety concerns. Whole muscle cuts such as a steak, a roast or a breast are only bacteria-colonized on their surfaces, making it easier to kill off any pathogens. Generally, bacteria are killed by cooking meat thoroughly, but that is a problem when it comes to a burger or a mechanically tenderized steak or roast. People like their beef or lamb rare or medium, and that just doesn't get the job done when it comes to killing off those unwanted hitchhikers. The industrial standard for safety in ground meat is 71°C (160°F). That temperature may render the product safe for consumption but a grey hockey puck is not what the diner is looking for when ordering or preparing a burger.

The additional danger in preparing any meat arises from the potential to cross-contaminate surfaces. Bacteria will cling to prep surfaces, knives, sponges and the hands of the preparer. The widespread habit of washing out a whole chicken, for example, will spread these bacteria all over the sinks and counters, anywhere the water from the chicken splashes. If a consumer or food preparer cuts meat and then vegetables without cleaning their knife or cutting board, cross-contamination will occur, and the likelihood of infection soars. By the way, *Salmonella* can survive for up to 72 hours on a dry surface and longer on a wet one. *Listeria* can multiply in the refrigerator. Sobering facts when it comes to keeping the food supply healthy.

The USA strives to be the leader in pioneering new technology for safe meat, but the EU is countering that with better on-farm hygiene and biosecurity. The incidences of disease from the 'favourite four' bacterial agents are roughly the same, with the EU seeing more campylobacteriosis and listeriosis than the USA.[13] Following the BSE epidemic, the EU has successfully harmonized food safety laws and regulations across the member states with a universal Food Law, adopted in 2002. Any country wishing to join the EU has to demonstrate its ability to adhere to the food safety practices demanded by the European Food Safety Administration (EFSA). Guidance for safety practices from farm to table is expected to be followed by all parties, and regular audits are conducted.

In the rest of the world, the figures on food-borne disease are far worse than those in the developed world. Indeed, in a comprehensive report published in 2005 by the Center for Science in the Public Interest,[14] it was reported that poorer or developing countries face a myriad of problems in the supply chain, causing major impediments to accessing safe food. The lack of safety measures also has an impact on their ability to trade with other countries. In addition, environmental toxins enter the food supply from industrial sources such as fertilizers or heavy metals, adding to the burden of food-borne disease in these populations. The lack of stability in government in many of these regions makes it impossible to implement meaningful food safety and handling laws. Food-borne illness is rampant through most of the developing world. We in the West should feel incredibly fortunate that we have the mechanisms not only to pass legislation but to enforce it as well. Most countries are not so lucky.

To illustrate that point, some estimates of food-borne illness in China suggest as many as 300 million cases per year.[15] But with data collection in China and many other developing countries hard to come by, it's difficult to know which of the probable causes is due to the four most common illnesses discussed here. In many cases, a failure to establish the basic cold chain required to safely store and transport meat and dairy products is the principal hindrance to the cause of safe food. Compounding that problem is lack of education in understanding how bacteria proliferate, contaminate and move from host to host. At the same time, where there are no barriers to moving products from region to region, bacteria are able to colonize new geographic areas, adding to the existing disease burdens.

Perhaps even more common than *E. coli* infection is salmonellosis, caused by the *Salmonella* bacteria. Discovered 125 years ago, this ubiquitous organism is estimated to cause over one million infections annually in the United States alone. In fact, the WHO estimates that tens of millions of people are affected yearly by salmonellosis.[16] Even those numbers are likely to fall far short of the reality since many people fail to report the illness, chalking it up to generic 'food poisoning' or 'stomach flu'. Similar to *E. coli*, *Salmonella* bacteria live in the intestines of animals and humans. Likewise an infection is most often acquired through contaminated food or water. It is particularly prevalent in chicken and in eggs, a development that has much to do with the intensive confinement model of poultry production. Other vectors for infection include milk, beef, pork and vegetables when they are sprayed with manure that has a high pathogen load of *Salmonella*. It is usually when people become ill in a cluster or, more rarely, when a processing facility conducts extensive testing that the bacteria are identified. In 2011 the meat giant Cargill recalled 35 million pounds (16 million kg) of ground turkey contaminated with *Salmonella* – and not just any old *Salmonella*.

To further complicate matters, *Salmonella* has evolved numerous new 'serotypes' that are resistant to one or more antibiotics. In the case of the Cargill recall, the serotype was *Salmonella* Heidelberg, a strain resistant to at least four commonly used antibiotics. Unlike *E. coli* where treatment with antibiotics is contraindicated, salmonellosis can require antibiotic treatment. As more strains become drug-resistant, the improper usage of antibiotics in the livestock industry clearly presents a public health emergency. A 2014 Consumer Reports study in the United States showed that 97 per cent of all chicken breasts they tested – more than 300 samples collected from stores across the nation – were infected with *Salmonella*, and many with the multidrug-resistant (MDR) strain called Heidelberg.[17]

The Europeans, particularly the Danish and the Dutch, have led the way in phasing out the prophylactic use of antibiotics, and as a result the incidence of MDR strains of food-borne illness has declined. The productivity of those industries suffered no significant economic impact from withdrawing the drugs when combined with improved vaccination programmes, probiotics and hygiene. With the support of the European governments, these modifications in husbandry protocols, while somewhat costly, were widely implemented. The EU system of using veterinarians as front-line observers of on-farm practices and slaughterhouse operations is very effective in promoting compliance with food safety measures. In addition, comprehensive data gathering on what antibiotics or antimicrobials are used in what quantities and where have further assisted the Danish and Dutch governments in identifying usage patterns from farm to farm.[18] Making sure that antibiotics are used *only* to treat illness, along with the other measures noted above, has resulted in the EU meat supply being safer, though people continue to fall ill. Their illnesses are not as virulent or difficult to treat and do not deliver the long-term damage seen from MDR bacteria.

Despite these successes, the USA, Brazil and China continue to regularly add antibiotics to the feed and water of their animals. The USA at present has no mechanism for tracking the use of these drugs in the livestock population beyond knowing how many pounds per year are sold. However, that may be changing. The FDA issued guidelines on how producers can use antibiotics on farms. The use of antibiotics as 'growth promotants' is being phased out, and by 2017 no farmer or producer will be able to introduce antibiotics to their animals without a veterinary prescription. In 2015 President Barack Obama signed the National Action

Plan for Combating Antibiotic Resistant Bacteria. Most of the measures are related to the healthcare system, but the use of antibiotics important to human medicine will not be allowed in livestock production to promote growth. Unfortunately, many producers will simply call their use of antibiotics 'disease prevention'. Indeed the use of antibiotics in the U.S. livestock industry has actually increased since the FDA guidances were issued in 2016. Additionally, the U.S. Congress has failed to allocate any funds for monitoring for compliance, so it is not at all clear how effective the guidelines or any further legislation will be in curbing the overuse of antibiotics in the livestock sector. Even with the industry trade organizations finally taking action to encourage producers to comply with a phase-out, progress has been painfully slow.

The third most common food-borne illness associated with meat and meat consumption is campylobacteriosis. Caused by the very common *Campylobacter* bacteria primarily found on poultry, this disease is estimated to affect 1.3 million people annually in the United States.[19] The EFSA believes it affects over nine million people in the EU and costs the EU a whopping €2.4 billion in lost productivity and medical care.[20] With all these food-borne illnesses, unless the case is unusually severe, requiring hospitalization or medications, the numbers reported are likely to be far below the actual incidence. Most people just take it in their stride when they have a stomach problem for a few days, no matter how unpleasant. Only when a community or multiple groups are affected can the government agencies responsible for public health identify a particular bacterium and trace it back to its source.

Listeriosis could be considered the fourth horseman of the food-borne illness apocalypse. *Listeria monocytogenes* is found more frequently in the developed world, thanks to its ability to withstand cold. The bacterium is most often associated with cold sliced meats, cheeses, sprouts and raw milk. Though a healthy adult will likely be only moderately affected by listeriosis, pregnant women are very much at risk, as are infants, young children, the elderly and the immune-compromised. According to the EFSA, listeriosis cases appear to be on the rise in the EU, while salmonellosis has declined.[21] The WHO is conducting a global study on listeriosis in an effort to better understand the disease and who is getting sick. The numbers they cite, while nowhere near as alarming as those associated with *E. coli* or *Salmonella*, are still impressive given the difficulty of correlating information on the disease from developing countries. Still, the WHO credited listeriosis with 23,150 cases, resulting in nearly 6,000 fatalities.[22]

There are two other alarming developments that have come about as a result of the excessive use of antibiotics in livestock operations. The first is the exponentially increasing numbers of people and livestock, especially pigs, testing positive for methicillin-resistant *Staphylococcus aureus*, or MRSA. This disease originated in hospitals as a result of the overuse of antibiotics. What has attracted scientists' attention is the evidence suggesting that community-acquired infections (such as from a hospital) have been successfully transferred to livestock operations. The animals may not get sick, but they do harbour the bacteria, and people who work in the industry are testing positive for MRSA in very high numbers. This is the first example of a disease that has gone from human to animal and back to humans; it is viewed as a real danger to the public.

Finally, over the last decade the incidence of urinary tract infections (UTIs) from drug-resistant *E. coli* has been observed in clinical settings.[23] In 2012 several papers published in the USA, Canada and the EU identified the same genetic fingerprints in drug-resistant *E. coli* from poultry as are found in human UTIs.[24] Some researchers suggest that it could be a human-to-animal transmission of drug resistance thanks to overuse of antibiotics in human medicine. Whatever the cause, the incidence of drug-resistant UTIs in humans is becoming a multibillion-dollar problem all over the world.

When people do get sick, the meat industry loves to point the finger at unsafe handling practices at home or in food service, rather than address the high bacterial loads on raw meat as it emerges from the processing facility. Many meat companies now include suggested cooking temperatures and stress safe handling on their labels. In reality, the recalls of millions of pounds of meat and the astonishing prevalence of food-borne illness in industrialized meat processing should signal to these major companies that their methods are less than adequate. Instead the blame for illness is most often laid at the door of the consumer, who lacks the hazmat suit and autoclave that would protect them from the irresponsible meat companies. To be fair, even organic meats processed outside of industrial-style facilities have plenty of bacteria on their surfaces. But drug-resistant bacteria are more likely to occur on industrially produced meat, and bacteria counts far exceed those found in small-scale production.

4
ENVIRONMENTAL COSTS

In order to understand how the environment is affected by CAFOs, it is essential to recognize their contribution to pollution through groundwater, air quality and soil degradation, in addition to the copious greenhouse gases they emit. In a 2013 report, the FAO identified livestock emissions as contributing roughly 14 per cent to greenhouse gases worldwide, but that figure is far from settled.[1] The marvellous efficiency offered by the CAFO model in producing food in record time with minimal inputs is completely offset by the environmental impacts of that same efficiency.

Imagine the plight of a pig farmer who has perhaps 10,000 pigs in each of his three or four big houses. Pigs in that concentration produce a lot of waste. There is an apocryphal tale that 10,000 pigs produce as much waste as a small city. But how accurate is that measure? According to a study from North Carolina State University (a heavy hog-producing state), it is really a comparison of apples to oranges, as human waste is heavily diluted with water before being swept to a water treatment plant where it is further treated and decontaminated.[2] That doesn't happen with animal waste. Moreover, depending on the size of the animal, one pig will excrete between 8 and 9.5 lb (3.6 and 4.3 kg) of manure a day.[3]

Multiply that by tens of thousands and it is easy to see that managing animal waste in the same fashion as human is simply not feasible without municipal-scale systems in place. Thus animal waste management has become a profoundly difficult problem to solve.

The current method for dealing with animal waste looks like this: manure and urine drop through slotted flooring where they are then mechanically swept out into a manure pit, or flushed out with water into a larger pit known as a lagoon. There it sits, generating methane, hydrogen sulphide and carbon dioxide along with a host of other volatile organic compounds (VOCs),[4] belching its foul odours and eye-watering ammonia into the atmosphere for all to breathe. That is the extent of the treatment for millions of pounds of faecal matter and urine in nearly all CAFOs around the world. Fatalities are not infrequent in farmers who are overwhelmed by those gases while attempting repairs or are otherwise trapped for too long in proximity to the manure receptacle. If an exhaust system fails in a pig or chicken house, the entire resident population can die in a matter of minutes thanks to the high concentrations of hydrogen sulphide.

Most farmers use some part of the waste-lagoon/manure-pit contents in a slurry that is sprayed on fields for fertilizer, but that consumes just a fraction of the overall supply. Using it as fertilizer comes with its own set of problems as well, and there are limits to how much can be deployed in this fashion at any one time. There are companies developing new ways of converting waste into denatured solids, cleaning the water or otherwise devising 'closed loop' systems where the waste can be used as fuel in the form of methane to power the facility. However, these systems cost in the millions and are obviously well out of reach of the average producer.

The smell, as anyone who has driven past a pig farm knows, is literally breathtaking. Though the aroma is primarily caused by hydrogen sulphide and ammonia, other gases are associated with intensive livestock production, including odourless gases such as methane and nitrous oxide. While bad smells may not seem life-threatening, the fact is that they are implicated in a variety of chronic lung disorders such as asthma and bronchitis, along with headaches, dizziness, hypertension, depression and even anxiety. Workers in CAFOs bear the brunt of the health assault, but surrounding populations document increased levels of disease caused by air quality issues.[5]

Technology abounds in strategies to mitigate those noxious odours: among them are air scrubbers, ozone flares, biofilters, fans, foggers and masking compounds. They can be deployed in any number of combinations, assuming the company responsible wants to take those measures. However, for a contract farmer with 50,000 pigs on his property, the costs of accessing and implementing the technology are formidable hurdles. The meat industry talks about becoming 'nose-blind', and presumably those working on a hog farm or in a rendering plant, where the most revolting of all the smells is produced, to a large degree do get used to it. Not so the surrounding communities, however. In the USA, noxious odours are considered a 'nuisance', and it can be a heavy lift to force a meat company to address the unpleasant aromas a facility emits. The general rule of thumb seems to be that if the smell strays beyond the perimeter of a facility, then a community can lodge a complaint with its local environmental department. Aside from that, the facility 'owns' the air within its acreage and above it as well. Smells don't recognize boundaries though, so when a breeze blows through it will take the smell with it. The problem for citizens seeking to report on an overwhelming stench is that, due to the vagaries of wind direction, frequently that terrible smell will be long gone before it has been documented. That makes it very hard to persuade a company to invest in the heavy artillery needed to mitigate the smells of a farm or a processing or rendering plant.

This is less of an issue in Europe where environmental impacts are tied to the direct payments farmers receive from the Common Agricultural Policy (CAP), the EU equivalent of farm subsidies. With limited land available for agriculture, the increased production of livestock on farm or in processing is discouraged beyond a certain size, mostly to prevent serious problems from odour, dust and waste. The better the environmental stewardship a farmer or grower can demonstrate, the higher their payments are likely to be from CAP. The EU has suffered the same growing pains as any other major producing region when it comes to managing manure and controlling water pollution.

In nations outside of the EU where there is more terrain, or a government more interested in promoting profit over environmental health, there are few if any measures citizens can take to protect themselves. It seems safe to assume that most rendering plants, processing facilities and CAFOs tend to take up space in areas that are populated by the less wealthy, less educated and least organized, thereby making it easier for companies to pollute with impunity.

Travelling on the wind along with those noxious gases are copious amounts of dust that are blown out of feedlots, or out of hog and chicken houses by their enormous ventilation systems. The dust is a heady mix of dried faecal matter, feed dust, animal dander or feather debris and dirt. Numerous studies suggest that the dust from feedlots and so forth could also be a vehicle for antibiotic-resistant bacteria,[6] among other components of what is called 'particulate matter' or PM. As this PM blows through an area, it sheds the larger particles, which can include manure inhabited by the 'food poisoning' bacteria we know so well, *E. coli*, *Salmonella* and *Listeria*, along with less common strains such as *Yersinia*, *Cryptosporidium* and *Giardia*.[7] Some scientists suggest that as the bacteria are blown together on the wind, they transfer genetic material, generating even more classes of MDR pathogens. No studies have conclusively demonstrated how far the dust travels, but the various components including endotoxins, and gut bacteria such as *Salmonella* or *Campylobacter*, have been shown to be able to survive for quite some time on land and in water.[8] There those multidrug-resistant microbes are absorbed by wildlife through the water, and by plants, including food crops, through the soil.

Until recently, in the USA the use of arsenic, a heavy metal, in controlling poultry disease was widespread. Arsenic is present in nearly all soil and water. What makes its use in livestock problematic is that as it passes through the digestive tract, it is converted from organic to 'inorganic' arsenic. Inorganic arsenic is a known carcinogen.[9] The practice of feeding arsenic to poultry led to an uptick in arsenic levels in groundwater and soil largely through the dissipation of PM from chicken operations. In addition, chicken 'litter' is also mixed with water and sprayed over cropland. Thus inorganic arsenic was discovered in all sorts of crops where it didn't belong, most notably the U.S. rice crop. Poultry litter is also a component of cattle feed. Though arsenicals were banned in EU poultry-producing countries in 1999, the industry favourite Roxazone was not banned in the USA until 2011. Nitarsone, the last remaining arsenical drug, has only been withdrawn from the American livestock market as of the end of 2015. Arsenic-based antimicrobials are still used extensively in China's mammoth broiler chicken and hog businesses. The presence of heavy metals in Chinese farmland can almost certainly be ascribed to the practice of using animal manure as fertilizer.

The WHO and the FAO have given some estimates on the use of antimicrobial/antibiotic use as growth promoters or AGP (antimicrobial growth promoter) overall in China, but they have not broken those numbers down into specific categories.[10] Numbers on the use of these drugs in worldwide livestock production are spotty at best, with the USA, in addition to China, having no mechanism for reporting on their use. India, Indonesia, Russia, Brazil and Argentina do not report on their use of antimicrobials either, yet they are all emerging as major producers in the never-ending expansion of the industry. As animals break down these drug compounds relatively inefficiently, there remains quite a bit of residue from them in their manure. Thus it is easy to see how the dust particulates glued to molecules of this huge class of drugs could ultimately have very dangerous consequences for human and animal health alike.

There have been few long-term studies on effects of PM on populations either working in or living near feedlots and swine and poultry houses, but research from numerous sources points out that it can and does have significant health impacts quite apart from the residual drugs and antibiotic-resistant bacteria.[11] What is less clear is why the industry, at least in developed countries, when confronted with these studies that conclusively demonstrate the dangers of the dust alone, largely chooses to ignore most recommendations for containing it. Air scrubbers in ventilation systems, walls, sprinklers and tree breaks are just a few options that could mitigate the health and environmental impacts of particulate dust from CAFOs. The cost of installation of these technologies is very substantial, and could only be borne by large corporations. But as more countries develop their own livestock industries, best practices should be shared, with international limits and regulations implemented by all countries. If all companies had to abide by the same environmental rules, countries with better laws would not be continually undercut in price by regions with none.

We have seen the impact of gas and dust on the environment. However, managing the wastewater from an intensive feeding facility is easily the most vital part of maintenance. Every strategy for waste management includes the application of the waste to cultivated fields as fertilizer. This would seem to be a brilliant way to restore fertility to depleted soils while disposing of some quantity of manure. Alas, the application of manure seems to far exceed the capacity of the soil to absorb so much nutrition at once, and run-off is an all too common problem. Even when the timing of those manure baths is regulated, it is an imperfect method. When it rains, the surface application of manure flows into any nearby body of water. If the manure is injected under the surface, the excess nutrients, primarily nitrogen and phosphorus, sink into the water table. Sometimes a pit or a lagoon will either rupture or overflow from heavy rain or flooding. When excessive amounts of nitrogen and phosphorus from manure wind up in waterways, it causes eutrophication or loss of oxygen in the water. Those two compounds will encourage the growth of great plumes of oxygen-depleting algae. This leads to massive fin and shellfish kills, along with a domino effect on other wildlife dependent on clean running water for habitat and food.

For several years the USA has experienced tremendous algae blooms from the nitrogen overload in the Great Lakes, affecting drinking water in cities such as Toledo, Ohio, located on Lake Erie. The Gulf of Mexico is home to a 'dead zone' measuring 5,000 square miles that is entirely due to agricultural runoff from the Mississippi River. The city of Des Moines, Iowa, located in a state of heavy corn and hog production, has taken the unprecedented step of suing upriver counties in an effort to force large-scale agricultural concerns to better manage their effluent. The drinking water for Des Moines comes from the Des Moines River and the Rocky River, both of which reek from chemicals and manure applied to fields upstream. Excessive nitrogen in the water is particularly dangerous to infants and young children, causing, among other problems, deadly 'blue baby' syndrome, where the baby, unable to absorb oxygen due to the excessive nitrogen, literally suffocates.

With the widespread use of manure for fertilizer, *E. coli*, *Clostridium botulinum*, *Salmonella*, *Giardia* and *Listeria* are travelling from the guts of livestock directly to fruits and vegetables that receive doses of manure from nearby feeding operations. Indeed, major food-borne illness outbreaks have been attributed to contaminated spinach, sprouts, melons and a host of other fresh non-meat products. This points to the dangers of using untreated manure from feedlots on farms that grow produce. Spraying or injecting manure slurry into farmland barely scratches the surface of the sheer quantity that needs processing and disposal. There are companies that employ powerful covered anaerobic digesters to manage faecal matter, but they are distinctly in the minority even in developed countries due to the high costs of installation and operation.

In countries such as China, with the largest confined pork population in the world, and the second largest of chickens, the disposal problem pretty much dwarfs all other issues associated with intensive livestock production. East Asia overall (China, Vietnam and Thailand) owns over half of the entire world population of pigs, and one-third of all poultry. In 2010 the Chinese government conducted an environmental survey and discovered some very alarming statistics. Agriculture actually outstripped heavy industry in creating pollution. Moreover, much of the manure, some 4.8 billion tonnes in 2008, the most recent figure available, was winding up in Chinese waterways. Sixty per cent of their groundwater is not safe for consumption![12] Much of their arable land has likewise been polluted with excess phosphorus, nitrogen and heavy metals. Meanwhile the industry is growing exponentially as the increasing affluence of the general population allows many more citizens to enjoy eating meat.

The FAO in conjunction with the World Bank and other entities has initiated projects in China, Vietnam and Thailand to address the pollution emanating from their expanding livestock operations. Anaerobic digesters, composting and other measures are being implemented, along with training and education. Chinese greenhouse-gas emissions from livestock and feed crop production are contributing tremendously to the overall global problems of climate change. Beginning in January 2016, the Chinese government has vowed to hand down stiff fines, closures and prison time to those who knowingly discharge waste or fail to manage their manure properly. It remains to be seen how compliant industry is with these new goals for environmental protection.

Possibly the most important aspect of environmental degradation from livestock is the production of food for all those animals. Most industrialized animal production relies heavily on two crops: soybeans and corn. In Central and South America, the clear-cutting of forest in order to grow more of these crops has generated justifiable alarm. In Central America alone, in 2005–6, 1.2 million hectares of forest were cut down to expand soy production.[13] Because of arcane land use rules and, frankly, widespread corruption, the pace of deforestation continues pretty much unabated. Specious deals between foreign and local companies have successfully found ways around land use legislation in order to put more land into the lucrative cultivation of the two feed crops.

Growing corn and soy in such great volumes has several unfortunate impacts. Firstly, both are very water-intensive crops. They require a tremendous amount of fertilizer in order to gain maximum production. More nitrogen and phosphorus from fertilizer means more nitrous oxide in the air and more water pollution from runoff. Clear-cutting forest for more pasture also releases enormous quantities of carbon dioxide into the atmosphere. On top of that, forest in Central and South America has been extensively cleared to make pasture for ruminants, such as cattle, which bring their own special contribution of methane to the party. No other region has created a more negative impact on indigenous habitat and populations than Latin America as a whole. There is also a major human factor in this equation. Turning all this land over to the service of corn, soy and cattle means less land to cultivate food for people. This conundrum of growing food for animals over people is the crux of the problem with industrialized animal production. There is not enough arable land on our planet to grow the food for 9.5 billion people come 2050 as well as the food for our burgeoning animal population.

As pork production swells, the EU is currently considering dropping a fifteen-year ban on swill feeding for pigs, a distinct step in the right direction. The ban was triggered by the disastrous outbreak of foot-and-mouth disease in 2002 in the UK. The outbreak seemed to be caused by feeding uncooked human food to pigs. However, other countries, most notably in East Asia and Japan, have been successfully feeding their pork populations with food waste for centuries. So, in a classic case of everything old is new again, it is dawning on producers that feeding omnivorous animals such as pigs with food wasted by humans could be a win–win for everyone. It is estimated that 102.5 million tonnes of food per year is wasted in the EU. If all that food were recycled into swill, farmers would save on feed costs, and global resources now allocated to growing corn and soy would be saved.[14] The Japanese even use the swill feeding of their pigs as a marketing tool, suggesting that they are more healthy and environmentally friendly than their corn-fed counterparts.

In 2006 the Livestock Environment and Development Initiative (LEAD), an inter-institutional consortium working out of the FAO, published a report called *Livestock's Long Shadow*. The report presented quite a grim picture of how growing animals for food is affecting the environment, populations and economies. LEAD continues to publish new assessments on climate change and the impact of livestock production as the numbers take off in parts of the world that have never before been meat eaters. Their reports offer many recommendations on how to mitigate the worst aspects of livestock production in relation to the planet.

How much or how well those recommendations are being implemented by individual governments is quite opaque, with some countries going well above and beyond in strategies to reduce their footprint, while others simply ignore or obfuscate their policies. The EU has an imperative to seek out new systems for growing livestock that does the least amount of harm to their environment because they have a relatively small amount of arable land on which to grow animals or feed. The USA, on the other hand, has ample resources, in addition to which the legislature is firmly held hostage by the combination of massive corporate interests that drive the meat industry. Latin American countries are also under the sway of corporate interests, evidenced by the continuing destruction of forest, displacement of indigenous farmers and willingness to cut deals with foreigners for growing the crops that feed meat production worldwide. India, Africa and East Asia struggle with similar issues as they do their best to insert themselves into world markets with little attention to the environmental costs of their meat business.

Fixing some of the environmental issues of growing meat is not an insurmountable problem. It is a problem of money and of political will. Managing excrement with infrastructure designed to denature its gases and bacteria just costs money. It absolutely can be done and some companies have already done it. Cargill Meat Solutions has a state-of-the-art processing plant in Fort Collins, Colorado, that has giant, covered, anaerobic digesters to manage all the wastewater from processing. The digesters cost them several million dollars to install, just a tiny drop from the Cargill pay bucket. The water is cleaned, and returned to the Colorado River. The harvested methane contributes to the company's power grid.

With governments pushing them, all the big players could implement the same type of technology for managing the waste of the business. As it stands, the model for industrial meat production is increasingly moving towards contract farming, where the company owns the genetics, the feed and the animals. The 'farmer' owns the facility in which the animals are fed and grown. He or she also owns their waste and their dead bodies. There is at present no mechanism whereby a company in contract with a farmer has any financial obligation to help to manage either waste or corpses. This system is neither fair, nor is it viable. Farmers are often served with lawsuits stemming from an inability to control odours, gases, waste and dust. Yet they are not paid nearly enough to install any but the most basic technology in order to mitigate these problems. Thus it is hardly surprising that the grow-out phase of livestock production is the one with the highest emissions. The highly profitable corporations responsible for the bulk of meat production in the world have successfully shifted responsibility for environmental degradation onto the shoulders of the contract workers and the surrounding communities. In fact, they should be slammed with massive lawsuits and fines for their failure to protect people and land from the by-products of their enormous profits.

5
ANIMAL WELFARE

In 1965 the British Government commissioned a report on animal husbandry in response to the intensification of livestock production. By 1979 that report, written by Professor Robert Bambrell, had become the backbone of animal welfare legislation that has subsequently been adopted by the World Organization for Animal Health, the Royal Society for the Prevention of Cruelty to Animals and the American Society for the Prevention of Cruelty to Animals. The report stated that in order to provide animals with a modicum of protection, they must have access to 'The Five Freedoms':

freedom from hunger or thirst by ready access to fresh water and a diet to maintain full health and vigour
freedom from discomfort by providing an appropriate environment including shelter and a comfortable resting area
freedom from pain, injury or disease by prevention or rapid diagnosis and treatment
freedom to express (most) normal behaviour by providing sufficient space, proper facilities and company of the animal's own kind

freedom from fear and distress by ensuring conditions and treatment which avoid mental suffering.

Since then, those standards have been disseminated around the world and many countries have signed pledges to uphold, at a minimum, those five freedoms. Indeed trade agreements can succeed or fail depending on the track record of a country's animal welfare scores. There are a number of agencies out there that are diligently monitoring compliance with not just the five basic freedoms, but with many ensuing issues around transportation and slaughtering protocols that have evolved with the growth of meat production. The World Animal Protection organization is perhaps the most involved. They advise the UN and the European Community on animal welfare issues. They also publish scorecards on the performance of more than fifty countries engaged in livestock production. The portrait they are able to paint shows a remarkable disparity in how that international pledge to animal welfare standards has played out.

Animal welfare in livestock production has gone from being something no one thought much about to a dominating factor in how many consumers choose their products. Most producers would say that they would never sabotage their own profits by mistreating animals, but that attitude is far from universal. Not every culture shares, for example, the predominately Western view that animals are 'sentient'. Not every culture recognizes that the quality of the end product is predicated on animal welfare – a hungry child is hardly going to complain about a tough piece of meat when meat is a rare luxury. Nevertheless, thanks to the trade implications of poor welfare, paying more attention to observing the basic standards set forth by the OIE (World Organization for Animal Health: Office International des Epizooties) is clearly an incentive for nations anxious to cash in on the world appetite for animal protein.

Western companies have spent millions on building and implementing humane slaughter methods. There are reams of papers written on the subject of animal welfare as it relates to stocking densities (animals per square inch or foot) in intensive operations. Millions of research dollars go into evaluating husbandry practices with a goal of promoting animal welfare to enhance their productivity. When animals are abused or neglected, too hot or too cold or subjected to poor air quality, or their feed is sub-par, they do not 'perform'. The industry continually directs its detractors to these efforts as its defence against accusations of cruelty. The USA 'outperforms' many other major producers, though virtually all its meat is grown in an industrialized setting. Its animals grow faster and are healthier than many of their counterparts, including animals that are more pasture-based. Clearly all that research has paid off to the extent that animals remain healthy and grow fast. But despite that success in 'productivity', the United States was awarded a 'D' in overall compliance with essential welfare concerns by the World Animal Protection Organization. Australia got a 'C', while the UK, France, Denmark, Austria and Germany were awarded 'As and Bs'.[1]

Thanks to the glut of stomach-churning videos captured by animal rights activists, the ugly truths behind the curtains of the meat business have slipped out. Whether meat-eaters or not, anyone who sees animals being abused certainly deplores the conditions whereby animals are made to suffer. And yet, if every feedlot or pig/poultry barn were to disappear and we went back to small-scale production, that would certainly be the end of the cheap meat so much of the world enjoys today. The question is, how much is the average consumer willing to pony up for meat raised to the minimum standard of the five freedoms, if not better?

Is just the very fact of confinement in and of itself cruel? Many people believe that is so. And yet, when animals are getting all the food and water they want, and living in relatively clean barns, kept warm, dry, and safe from predators, they probably think that overall they have it pretty good. But it is also true that depending on the species, and even the breed, confinement can present a host of miseries that do deserve to be rectified. All livestock species have 'normal behaviours', or the behaviour they would be practising on small-scale farms. For this reason, one of the 'Five Freedoms' is just that – freedom to express (most) normal behaviours. The industry identifies the fact that cattle, sheep, pigs and poultry are all very reliant on herd behaviour as evidence that they like to be kept close together. In a normal farm setting it keeps them safer from predators. Furthermore all of those species are sociable, and elaborate social hierarchies are formed within fixed groups. However, those hierarchies are continually disrupted in an industrial setting, as animals are moved in and out of housing destined for slaughter. Added to that is the number of animals kept in one space. The guidelines for those stocking densities vary widely from country to country, and can account for much of what is identified as 'inhumane'.

It goes without saying that animal welfare in any setting is highly dependent on the people involved in caring for those animals, whether in the grow cycle or in the processing arena. Compliance with rules on how to treat, move and otherwise handle livestock is extremely difficult to monitor for any government agency, and most of the responsibility for that monitoring is placed in the hands of the individual company or enterprise. Lack of funding, lack of oversight and poor training in handling are the principal causes of animal abuse. Moreover, the onus to produce and process swiftly and efficiently causes many companies to ignore problems unless there is an incidence of consistently poor product that lowers profits, or cruelty is caught on camera by an activist. Poor animal welfare on farm, in transit or at the processor will result in lower-quality end results. Frightened or abused cattle show up as 'dark cutters' because of the excess cortisol in muscles. In pigs, the result will be 'pale, soft, exudative' meat or 'dark, firm and dry meat', industry-speak for crummy pork. Chickens suffer more from bruising and broken limbs, which can exclude them from the supply line as anything other than ground (minced) meat. Because these qualities lower the value of the product, the industry continually uses the economic incentives conferred by humane practices to defend itself from charges of cruelty.

Though they are now being phased out of most production practices around the world, the use of gestation crates and farrowing stalls in raising pigs has attracted a great deal of unwanted public attention. Farmers defend the use of farrowing stalls where the sow gives birth and suckles, because it protects the piglets from being crushed by the mother. The gestation crate keeps pregnant sows from fighting over food, as they are prone to do in group housing when there are too many animals in one space. Gestation crates became very popular with farmers in the 1980s and '90s when the industry consolidated and most pork production was moved indoors. Prior to that, pigs were raised outdoors, with barns or hoop houses for shelter. Because the gestation crate allows the producer to precisely calibrate the food for a sow, it is seen as a valuable tool in helping her to produce healthier piglets and to recover faster from pregnancy, birth and lactation so she can be bred again . . . and again . . . and again.

But keeping a breeding sow in a cage for the majority of her days for the benefit of the producer is clearly inhumane. Many countries, including Canada and much of the EU, have already phased out the practice. Contrary to conventional theory, productivity in sows has been shown to increase when they are kept in group housing instead of gestation crates. Only nine states in the USA have committed to phasing out gestation crates, but as more major food retailers such as McDonald's, Whole Foods and other companies demand crate-free pork products, it is safe to assume that they will soon be a thing of the past. Even WH Group/ Smithfield, the giant among pork producers, committed itself in 2009 to eliminating gestation crates from their producers by 2022.

In the case of farrowing crates, keeping a sow confined in an area so the piglets have access to the teats, but won't be squashed when the sow moves, makes a lot of sense to a farmer whose piglet mortality rate is a defining factor in profitability. This is something most people can understand. In addition, piglets need more warmth than the mother, so farrowing crates have a separate additional source of warmth to keep them at their optimum temperature. It is also true that sows in group housing experience more piglet mortality. Still, they are able to engage in reasonably normal social behaviour. Newer and ongoing research in animal behaviour, as measured by performance in feed conversion, that is, growth and weight gain, as well as reproductive capacities, is beginning to show the imperative of permitting natural behaviours as an economic strategy instead of treating animals like widgets.[2] Producers who have invested heavily in farrowing or gestation structures often cannot change their housing overnight and many more will not change their minds. Some still believe that keeping animals segregated and confined increases productivity instead of recognizing it as torture to highly sociable, curious and communicative creatures.

The happiest pigs are those allowed to engage in the full range of normal pig behaviour: socializing, the all-important rooting, foraging, wallowing, nest-building when ready to give birth, and just plain walking around, an activity that is totally absent in any intensive setting. If confined to an indoor setting, pigs like to play with toys, and best practices include giving them 'stimulation', as in objects they can kick or toss, chew on or play tug of war with. A bale of straw will keep a pen of pigs pretty happy. When pigs are kept in close confinement and do not have something to do besides eating and sleeping, they fight, bite each other's tails and ears, and otherwise exhibit aggressive and dangerous behaviours that can result in injury to themselves, other pigs or the people working around them. That behaviour alone demonstrates the folly of depriving them of their natural activities.

Poultry are also the subject of scrutiny from animal welfare activists, and for good reason. In the USA, animal welfare law was written to include only cattle and swine. Poultry have no protections. The same was true in the EU until welfare regulations were imposed in 2007. Many companies have now committed to 'cage-free' eggs thanks to consumer outrage over the practice of keeping birds in very small 'battery' cages where they cannot engage in their natural behaviours such as roosting, preening, scratching and dust-bathing. Less attention is paid to their brethren, the broilers, or 'meat birds'. Broilers have the same needs, in terms of natural behaviours, as layers. Most broiler operations raise their birds in giant barns growing from chick to chicken in a brief span of some 45 days. They have quite a lot of room in the chick phase, but by the time they reach market weight they are packed in together, allowing for minimum movement, and certainly less ability to exhibit natural behaviours, though this depends greatly on stocking densities.[3]

There are other factors that affect the birds as they grow out, including how much or little light they are subjected to. Encouraging them to eat more at certain times and less at others during their grow-out, the amount of 'daylight' is heavily manipulated. There is also the matter of the genetic selection of today's conventional broiler. Growing from egg to table in less than two months has serious welfare consequences. The breast of our favourite bird is much too heavy for those barely formed skeletons to hold them up. Even if those chickens are grown outdoors in plenty of room, by the time they are meat they can hardly walk. In fact, 'gait scores' are a major means of identifying welfare problems. Improving gait scores can be addressed by stocking densities, and improvements can be made all the way back to how the egg is incubated and even what genetics are in play when the egg is fertilized. All of these elements affect the overall welfare of the broiler chicken. Not surprisingly poultry exhibit many of the same unhealthy behaviours that can be observed in any livestock species when jammed into a small space with too many animals. They become aggressive and will bite and peck one another, and yank out feathers, causing pain, infections and frequent mortality in the victim.

Cattle are also stressed by overcrowding. Cows need to lie down often, especially the dairy breeds. They like to groom each other too. They like to graze. When those behaviours are curtailed or eliminated, cows will engage in a variety of behaviours such as tongue-rolling, mouthing or munching on fencing and gates, or throwing their food around (particularly annoying to someone paying for that food). They will bully other cows, and both male and female will exhibit mounting behaviour. In general, beef cattle spend less time in intensive confinement than other meat animals (this is not true of dairy cattle who are confined for much of their milking lives), so their welfare issues stem mostly from fear and distress due to bad handling, failure to protect them from inclement weather, and infection and disease from dirty confinement systems.

In all it seems pretty clear that jamming any species into spaces too small to accommodate their numbers has negative impacts on the well-being of those animals. So the balance between full-on misery and tolerable discomfort has been very carefully calibrated by the industry.

Then there are the 'industry practices' which, when revealed to the consumer, cause considerable consternation. And yet they are stoutly defended by the industry. Tail-docking, beak-clipping, tooth-clipping, castration (all frequently performed without anaesthesia), nose rings and a host of other interventions are measures typically described by industry insiders as designed to enhance animal welfare by cutting down on undesirable behaviours that can lead to disease and death.

Studies on the widespread use of beak-trimming have shown that the bird may live out the rest of its life in constant pain, especially if the technique is poorly practised or done with older-style equipment. Nowadays many birds are trimmed with infrared, a technique that appears to diminish the pain felt by the animal. That is not an industry-wide practice, and many hatcheries will use a hot knife or clippers. Similarly, the removal of pigs' tails can also cause pain for the rest of that animal's life.

Still, clipping a beak and docking a tail prevent pecking and tail-biting on a large scale, so those practices seem clearly justified to producers. It is worth noting that if animals were offered enough stimulation in the form of engaging in 'natural behaviours' they probably would not be expending energy on biting and yanking. However, it would appear that many producers feel more comfortable with altering the animal's physical characteristics than making the commitment to promote stress-relieving natural behaviours.

Some interventions are clearly pretty essential, and legislation in many countries mandates the use of anaesthesia or analgesics on older animals. Some of the interventions are performed when the animal is very young, such as 'polling' cattle, a procedure that cauterizes horn buds and prevents the animal from developing horns that may cause problems later in life. Genetic selection for traits such as 'polled' sheep or cattle is heavily studied and promoted as solutions for potential serious welfare problems in animals confined in close quarters with not enough to do except eat, sleep and turn into meat. Many of these 'industry practices' inflict significant pain and suffering in the service of the system. The 'industry practice' argument legitimizes the suffering of animals, when in fact most of these interventions are tools for the industry to maintain profitability and ease of management. Still some of them are hard to argue with, since clearly a sharp horn in the eye or the gut is going to hurt badly, as is being pecked and de-feathered, or having an ear or tail chewed off by an angry pig. Meat production is so fraught with ethical and humane issues it can hardly be surprising that animal welfare is the most polarizing aspect of the entire business.

To make a last point on industry practices, few people recognize the impact of feeding grain to cattle, an animal uniquely unqualified to thrive on that kind of diet. Cows have multiple-chambered stomachs, the first chamber being the rumen. Because cows are grass feeders they need to break down the cellulose in grass and hay, and that is the job of the rumen. When they are put on to a grain diet, the sugars in grains such as corn, barley and wheat speed up the fermentation process and cause sub-acute or acute acidosis. The acute onset can result in death. It's a huge problem for the feedlot, and tinkering with the diet is pretty near constant in order to achieve that fast growth and intramuscular fat that is conferred by eating grain, while trying to control the production of acid that discourages the animal from eating at all. Acidosis has been shown to contribute to other significant problems such as liver abscess and acute interstitial pneumonia, two very debilitating conditions. In short, the industry standard of finishing cattle on grain means that the animals are forced to suffer for months from a stomach ache, if not worse.

Then there is the matter of drugs. Not just the antibiotics, which do keep animals healthy in confinement even as they stimulate growth. There are other drugs deployed to increase speed of growth, and none is more controversial than beta agonists. They have been banned in the EU, China and even Russia. In fact, 160 countries have banned this class of drug in livestock production. The EU tends to be conservative about using drugs in livestock production anyway, and particularly if there may be a danger to the humans consuming their meat. While there have been no definitive ties to human illness from meat tainted with beta-agonist residues, enough questions about its safety remain. In addition, the high animal welfare standards common to the EU present an obvious case for rejecting these drugs because of the implications of negative impacts on the animals. For China and Russia, however, countries where animal and human welfare would appear to be less of a priority, there must be a significant reason to ban a potentially useful drug. Despite the widespread antipathy to the use of this class of growth promotants, the USA, Brazil, Canada, Mexico and some 22 other countries continue to use it. The drugs ractopamine and zilpaterol are used in hog, poultry and cattle operations.[4]

Due to the requirements of trading partners, some companies are voluntarily segregating herds and flocks into groups that don't get beta agonists and those that do. The USA, in particular, vigorously defends their use, protesting that residues in meat are negligible and pose no threat to consumers. Instead, the U.S. meat companies and the U.S. pharmaceutical lobby insist that the ban on the use of beta agonists is a 'trade protection' measure aimed at keeping American meat out of international markets. Nevertheless, even before the Chinese acquired pork giant Smithfield, or perhaps in anticipation, beta agonists were withdrawn from the Smithfield pork supply slated for the Asian markets. Other companies, such as Cargill and Tyson, have voluntarily elected to phase out their use in their operations.

Animal welfare activists do not take such a benign view of beta agonists, which were initially developed to control asthma in humans. They do help animals produce more lean meat, hence their appeal to the meat industry, but they have also been implicated in higher mortality figures and just plain ill health. Ractopamine is suspected of being particularly damaging to pigs, which appear to experience cardiac problems, trembling, aggressive behavioural problems and mobility issues. Eyewitness reports state that ractopamine can cause cattle hooves to fall off, in addition to making cows fall down. Most notably, animals treated with beta agonists seem to fare far worse than their untreated cohort when subjected to stress, particularly the stress associated with transportation. A 2014 study conducted by animal scientists from Texas Tech University and Kansas State University reported increased mortality in animals fed beta agonists. However, Elanco, one of the manufacturers, dismissed the study as inconclusive, saying that it was 'based on observational information versus rigorous, randomized scientific evaluation . . . so drawing conclusions from such analysis should be done with caution.'[5] Clearly the use of beta agonists is a controversial issue inside the industry, as well as to animal welfare advocates and public health organizations.

Most people worry about the use of hormones in meat animals. Only cattle and sheep are given hormones. The dairy industry relies on one hormone in particular, rBGH, to induce cattle to produce prodigious quantities of milk, far beyond the normal supply of any milker. The fact that it also induces a high incidence of painful mastitis did not seem to figure in the deliberations of the FDA when its use was first proposed in 1993 in the United States. Most other dairy-producing countries have banned its use, but the USA seems to see no problem with it. According to the Humane Society of the United States (HSUS), 90 per cent of feedlot-finished cattle are given one of several growth-promoting hormones.[6] Australia relies intensively on hormone use in its cattle, primarily because the majority of them are pasture-raised throughout their lives, with no other growth promotants such as low-dose antibiotics. Thus it would take significantly longer for its cattle to come to market weight without them, conferring considerable economic advantage on competitors who exploit every means of moving their animals along the production path swiftly.

According to that same Humane Society report of 2016, European scientists identified a plethora of possible adverse impacts on human health from the use of growth hormones in meat animals. The list included neurobiological, immunological, developmental and reproductive effects, as well as some carcinogenic properties. The drugs remain in wide circulation despite the number of countries that have banned their use.

Transportation

Consumers don't often consider the journeys that animals take from farm to feedlot or feedlot to slaughterhouse. But transportation is a critical element of animal welfare, and millions of animals a year die in transit due to injury, stress, heat, cold or poor ventilation. Many more endure significant injuries from broken limbs, bruising or trampling. In long-distance hauling, the number of hours an animal can be kept on a truck without rest is regulated, but policing is difficult even in the EU, where animal welfare regulations are more stringent than in any other region in the world.[7]

The USA still complies with the 28-hour rule, adopted in 1873, and subsequently updated in 1904 and most recently in 1994. At the time the rule was adopted it was primarily directed at the cattle markets in an era when cattle were being transported by rail from the West to Chicago, Kansas City and New York. It wasn't until 2004 that the rule was amended to reflect the fact that 95 per cent of all livestock in the USA are now moved by truck. The United States Department of Agriculture (USDA) did not make that fact public until 2007 when pressured by animal rights activists.[8] After 28 hours of transportation, animals must be allowed to rest for five hours at a minimum, and given food and water. By contrast, transportation rules in the EU mandate a maximum journey of eight hours, with an additional two-hour allowance if near enough to the destination to make unloading the animals for rest an additional stressor.

Depending on the country or region, animals are allowed water during transport, but feed is kept at a minimum, if not eliminated altogether. The ideal is for animals to arrive in a fairly clean state, as their manure will shed more bacteria such as *Salmonella* when they are stressed out in transit. Because manure then clings to the hides, every effort is made to keep them from getting too dirty in transit. Animals are not washed or cleaned before processing, and, if the hide is filthy, there is a far greater risk of contamination from any one of the major food-borne pathogens including *E. coli*, *Salmonella* and *Campylobacter*.

The rules for watering vary enormously from one country to another. In Australia, water can be withheld for as long as 48 hours for cattle, 24 for sheep and twelve for pigs, the last the most vulnerable to transport stress.[9] Ambient temperatures outside and inside the truck, along with how many animals are packed into a vehicle, contribute to either causing or alleviating stress. Conveyances for livestock are frequently inadequate in controlling temperature and ventilation, especially in developing countries. Even in the USA, figures for mortality due to transportation show that an estimated U.S.$50–100 million is lost annually by the pork industry alone.[10]

Despite new techniques in satellite monitoring of trucks, and a better understanding of how transportation affects the health of livestock, no one engaged in the business has figured out how to completely offset the impacts of travel, whether over long or short distances. In less developed countries the problems are compounded by lack of infrastructure for loading and unloading stock, along with incompetent, untrained personnel, bad drivers and worse roads, and poorly designed trucks with improper flooring that causes falls and trampling. The consolidation of processing houses from local nearby facilities to larger plants at greater distances has contributed enormously to this problem. Australia and New Zealand export sheep to the Middle East via boat, a factor that has led to horrific animal welfare disasters with significant mortality, starvation and infection.[11] Animal welfare overall would benefit greatly from a return to localized slaughter in inspected plants and the transportation of carcasses rather than live animals.

The final piece of the equation is the human factor. To quote Dr Temple Grandin, the animal behaviour scientist and author,

> only about 20% of the people working with livestock are natural stockmen. Then there is a whole middle ground of people who can be supervised and trained, and then the bottom 10% just should not be handling cattle, they like to hurt them and should not be there.[12]

No country has a monopoly on best practices, just as no country has a monopoly on cruelty. According to industry leaders, the success of any livestock operation is dependent on the well-being of the animals and the successful husbandry carried out by the employees who handle them. If that is truly the case, one must ask why so many videos have surfaced that indisputably demonstrate that animal welfare protocols are not being observed. Every time an animal welfare advocacy group such as People for the Ethical Treatment of Animals (PETA) or the HSUS manages to catch some egregious act of cruelty, the industry always points to 'one bad actor' or 'one rotten apple'. This is a gross understatement of what amounts to industry-wide failure to adequately train and supervise workers in the proper handling of livestock.

In the absence of detailed government regulations on animal slaughter, Dr Grandin wrote the manual that has been adopted by the American Meat Institute and which has been widely emulated throughout the industry abroad. With her unique understanding of animal behaviour and perceptions, she has assisted the meat industry enormously by designing facilities that help to move the animals with less stress, developing methods for loading and unloading stock and for moving them through the stunning box safely and humanely. To be fair, though it is from large plants or operations that those horrible videos most often surface, they are not alone when it comes to a breakdown in animal handling. The FSIS, or Food Safety and Inspection Services branch of the USDA, publishes quarterly reports on various food safety issues including 'inhumane handling'. The majority of offenders tend to be in small and medium-size abattoirs that probably lack the financial means, if not the will, to implement the infrastructure and training that would bring animal welfare up to the standards published by the industry itself.

Training, management, auditing by a third party, and the funding of government muscle in supervising the meat industry would enormously improve the lot of animals destined for food. However, without a society that views animal welfare as a critical aspect of the supply chain, it is axiomatic that cruelty will remain a significant element of the industry.

In a fascinating survey produced by the World Animal Protection Organization, the question was posed, 'Are there economic or societal barriers to improving animal welfare in the country?' Fifty different countries were appraised on this basis, and the results were predictably mixed. Russia, for example, was awarded this evaluation:

> There is no evidence of human and financial resource allocated to promote animal protection or animal welfare. This does not appear to be a government priority. A general lack of concern for animal welfare in society appears to act as a significant barrier to progress with respect to animal welfare.

The USA garnered this *mot juste*:

> It is positive that the United States approach is to involve stakeholders in the development of legislation. However, the adversarial approach to policy and

> legislation development; the strength of commercial lobbies opposed to measures increasing animal protection; and measures that inhibit or prevent public exposure of animal suffering in agricultural production represent considerable barriers to progress.[13]

Clearly there is a vast disparity in how the industry is perceived and regulated across the nations. Placing the policing of animal welfare into the hands of a profit-driven industry is highly problematic. Just as clearly, these evaluations show that development and enforcement of animal welfare protocols must be driven by strict government regulations, with appropriate funding and the power to punish or shut down industry players with bad practices. Currently the leaders in enforcement are all in the EU, where veterinarians are used as inspectors both on farm and in slaughter plants. They are fully independent and can operate without fear of retaliation or termination, which is not the case in the USA and other countries.

To quote Dr Grandin again, 'The responsibility for animal welfare lies with management.' If a farm or plant is well managed then the animals will be at least treated well enough to feel comfortable and to be clean and well fed. What is happening in the industrialized model is that management is more engaged with profit than with welfare, two aspects frequently at odds with one another, despite the claims to the contrary so often repeated by industry insiders.

In the next chapter, we will examine the labour issues that contribute to animal welfare failures.

6
WAGES, WORKERS AND SAFETY ISSUES

The International Labor Organization (ILO), a specialized agency of the United Nations, has codified labour practices that guarantee certain rights for workers, no matter the industry. Among them are freedom of association; collective bargaining and industrial relations; the abolition of forced labour; equality of opportunity and treatment; employment security and protection of wages; hours of work; weekly rest and paid leave; occupational safety and health; and employment injury benefits.[1] Though many countries may have laws that reflect those standards on their books, research has shown that what's on the books frequently is not matched in practice. Within the meat-processing industry, there has been a race to the bottom as the globalization of the food supply makes it easy for one nation to undercut another in trade simply by exploiting its workers. This is very much the norm in the American, European, Australian and South American meat-processing industries.

In the first half of the twentieth century meat processing was a steady and lucrative job that supported a family, and bound together the towns and communities centred around a plant. Meat processing, or packing as it is also known, formed part of the backbone of the industrial food supply.

This was true in the USA, Australia and throughout Europe. Nowadays, the average U.S. meatpacking job pays an average of $11 an hour, down from the nearly $20 an hour of the 1960s and '70s negotiated by the United Packing House Workers of America, an early meatpackers' union. Australians are desperately hanging on to an hourly rate that can reach as much as A$32 an hour, affording the middle-class existence that once characterized the industry. The EU offers wages that vary widely depending on which member state is being examined. The pay is highly dependent on whether or not immigrant labour is used, and how much government oversight is directed at the industry.

In the USA, EU and Australia, labour laws and/or the right to unionize once guaranteed decent wages, basic benefits such as paid sick leave or vacation, and occupational safety rules that protected workers against injury. Over the last three to four decades those guarantees have been curbed or eliminated. What caused the erosion of fair labour practices in the industry?

While meatpacking was taking place in urban settings, near distribution hubs and big markets, there was no shortage of skilled labour to man those plants. Once the plants began moving closer to the animals, as in feedlots, or intensive operations (to minimize the transport of live animals), it became more of a challenge to acquire the experienced workers needed to break down the animals. To compensate for the loss of skill, meat processing was subjected to the Henry Ford model of mass production, or in this case, deconstruction. Every cut made to dismember an animal and reduce it to pieces was studied, its place in the process examined, and efficiencies in the movement of the worker and the carcass identified. Deconstructing the animal cut by cut meant that the skill of a trained meatpacker was no longer a determining factor in harvesting a maximum profit. It also meant that an unskilled worker could often be substituted for one with training, experience and seniority. This development alone essentially sounded the death knell for the butchering trade as it once existed.

The movement out of the urban environment also meant that the trade unions advocating for workers lost significant membership as the employment opportunities for skilled workers dwindled. In the place of those skilled workers, companies began to recruit locally from the towns in which the processing plants set up shop. As the unions lost members, their power to negotiate good wages and benefits diminished. Without union protections, local people dropped out of the employment pool. Companies began soliciting, and even importing, workers from elsewhere who were more willing to do the dangerous, dirty work of cutting up animals. Beginning in the 1980s an industry-wide move to reduce the power of unions was adopted, especially in the USA and Australia, part of an overall political philosophy that was geared towards employers rather than employees.[2]

In the United States, the quest to de-unionize led to companies threatening to idle or close a plant to force workers to take lower wages and benefits. In many cases they made good on the threat to shut down, opening up a few months later under a new name and without a union contract. With no union on premises the company has the freedom to hire exclusively non-union employees.

The breakdown and marginalization of unions in meatpacking has allowed companies to cut costs extensively by reducing wages and benefits, leading to increased profit. Even when labour laws presumably guarantee certain rights and freedoms, as they do in the USA, EU, Australia, South America and China, the enforcement is lax at best. In the same way as the USA has largely replaced American workers in meat production with immigrants, Australia is importing 'guest' workers from all over Asia.

The European Union continues to support basic workers' rights in the way of a liveable wage, paid leave and compensation for injuries. Nevertheless the American model is infiltrating, with German and UK plants, in particular, sourcing workers from less affluent parts of the EU as 'guest' workers who are willing to take far less in pay and benefits. A recent report on German labour exposed the fact that many of their meatpacking workers are paid less than €8.50 per hour.[3] Using labour contractors, companies import workers from EU countries such as Poland and Romania. The 'gangmaster', as labour contractors are called, often misrepresents the wage and the living conditions for imported workers, promising one thing but delivering another once the worker has left home and country and signed a contract. In another scenario a plant will enter into a production contract with a foreign company which is then allowed to import its own workers to do the work. The foreign company can pay what it normally pays without any obligation to observe local requirements for wage or benefits. This model has come to dominate production in Germany.[4] By contrast, France pays its meatpackers 17 per cent more than Germany, and

Denmark pays 42 per cent more for the same labour. Austria, Belgium and France have all complained at various times to the governing body of the EU that Germany's low wage is forcing some of their own businesses to close, unable to compete with the low prices generated from paying next to nothing for labour.[5]

Brazil's meat industry has been accused of nothing less than slavery in the way it dupes and steals from its workers. Reports from multiple news media and humanitarian agencies expose scenarios that make the 'gangmasters' of the EU and Australia look fluffy by comparison. Workers report having their documents seized and their wages withheld, being forced to pay for food and housing whose costs exceed their earnings and worse. The prevalence of strikes in Brazil for wages and for basic safety protocols are frequent enough to illustrate the poor conditions in which most meat workers toil.[6]

Aside from the low wages and hard work, the meatpacking industry is notorious for its dangers. Some improvements have been made, but fatal accidents, and amputations, remain fairly common. Industry has invested heavily in processes to prevent people from disappearing into giant meat grinders, but in fact those accidents still happen. A major improvement is in the required safety gear for meat cutters. Most cutters wear steel mesh gloves, and sleeves, and mesh or leather aprons to protect from knife accidents. Footwear, helmets, ear protection, goggles, and in some cases even respirators, are required, along with rubber boots, gowns and other gear. The gear is provided by the company and must be kept up to date and replaced when damaged.[7]

All that gear is heavy and cumbersome, and takes quite a while to put on and take off. Many a lawsuit has been brought against meatpacking companies over the issue of pay for 'donning and doffing', with as yet no industry standard for workers being paid for that time. Typically workers have to bring a lawsuit in order to be compensated for the daily hour or more it takes to put on and take off their job gear. If there is no union in the shop, that time is never paid for.

The dangers from heavy equipment and knives are dwarfed by what really makes the profession so hazardous: repetitive motion. Imagine making the exact same motion in exactly the same way 20,000 times. Imagine doing that in one day. Such is the life of the line worker in a meatpacking plant. The musculoskeletal damage due to repetitive motion is the root cause of most long-term, serious injuries in the industry.

The ergonomics of those motions are the subject of numerous studies designed to try to engineer out the damage to the worker's body, but so far to little avail. In 2000 the U.S. Occupational Safety and Health Administration passed ergonomic standards to relieve some of those issues from the production line; however, the measures were repealed by the industry-friendly Bush Administration in 2001. In order to combat the stress of repetitive motion, workers would have to be moved from station to station along the line all day. With a ready supply of disposable non-skilled workers, the industry absorbs sometimes as much as 100 per cent turnover per year. Thus there is little incentive for management to disrupt the production flow in order to protect their workers.

Few countries' industries have the kind of capacity that characterizes the United States where the daily processing of thousands of cattle, and tens of thousands of pigs or chickens, is the norm rather than the exception. The European Union still has relatively small processing plants where the number of animals moved through remains in the hundreds per day, not the thousands that are typical in Brazil, the USA and Australia. Up until recently, the EU's export of meat was pretty well confined within European borders. However, as new trade deals emerge, the movement of goods, including meat, out of the EU and across borders to new trading partners will undoubtedly unleash a major expansion in processing.

Let's talk for a minute about the line, or 'chain' as it is more commonly called. Here is a quick sketch of how this disassembly process works in virtually any packing house, with obvious differences for the type of processor. Poultry processing is not going to reflect anything like the same level of peril for a worker as is common in a cattle or pork plant, but it too has its own special dangers which will be addressed later. A cattle plant is easily the most hazardous, thanks to the size and weight of the animal and the machinery involved in its processing.

Here is how it works: a cow goes into the stunning box, where it gets hit in the head with a six-inch captive bolt stunner, rendering it insensible. It goes down, and another worker immediately passes a hook into the animal's ankle by which it is hoisted up on a rail. There it is stuck in the neck, and bleeds out in a matter of seconds. When done well, this method works perfectly, with little if any pain or fear experienced by the animal.

This method owes its efficacy to Dr Temple Grandin, who not only designed much of the system but devised a scoring method to ensure compliance. Once the animal is on the rail, it moves to another station to have its hide pulled, along with other processes that remove the hoofs, head, tail and rectum. Then the animal is eviscerated. The worker who mans the evisceration of the animal holds a position that one Cargill plant director described as the 'rockstar' of the cutters. Indeed it is truly tricky to empty the contents of a carcass without nicking an intestine, stomach or rumen that could spill out pathogen-laden contents. Next the carcass goes up on a rail again, where it is cut in two by men who balance on a swinging plank wielding chainsaws, and whose job is to cut *exactly* down the spinal cord so as to remove any possible neurological tissue, a source of BSE. Once the animal is cut in half, it is chilled, and then arrives on the fabrication floor where it is first cut into 'primals' such as the chuck, loins, round and ribs. Further on, those big primals are broken into the cuts that we find in the supermarket. The cutters stand cheek by jowl. The noise from the heavy machinery is deafening and workers must wear ear protection. The entire cutting room is chilled to help prevent the growth of pathogens and bacteria. At the same time there is an ever-present cloud of steam from the boiling-hot water and cleaning solutions used to sanitize knives and equipment as the carcasses pass through. The opportunities for injury are legion at every station in the process. Whether it's dealing with the enormous saws and grinders, the rapidly moving knives, or the sheer weight of the carcasses and chunks as they sail through on their automated journey to the supermarket, the entire arena is an accident waiting to happen. The floors are wet and greasy from fat, blood and water, so slips and falls are very common.

Now imagine that this whole process occurs 400 times or more in an hour. Some cattle-processing plants can move more than 4,000 animals in two eight-hour shifts. Pork processing can move at speeds of up to 16,000 animals per eight-hour shift. This is what is called a high chain speed, and absolutely nothing in this process lends more danger to the entire venture than a high chain speed. It raises the odds of cuts, accidents and repetitive motion injuries exponentially. However, chain speed is what drives profit. The faster the animal is turned into neat little packages of meat, the less it costs per unit, and the higher the return for the company.

In many plants, the incidence of accident or injury is linked to the success or failure of a manager or supervisor whose primary concern is to meet his or her production quotas. Therefore a worker who wants to keep his job also learns to keep his trap shut for fear of retaliation by a supervisor for interrupting the production line with a problem or request. Shutting down the line for any reason, including food safety, is frowned upon, and even USDA inspectors are wary of making too many demands around quality. Despite the 'labour right' to report injury and expect medical care, the reality is that few workers will risk doing so until or unless that injury prevents them from performing their duties. Frequently the industry will demand that workers put in an extra hour or two in order to finish processing that day's slaughter. They do not typically receive overtime pay for that time, another abrogation of a labour right. Studies have shown that most accidents and injuries occur during those last few hours of a shift, especially the extra hours when workers tend to be tired anyway or, even more likely, in pain. Nevertheless, companies force workers to remain on the job or face penalties or termination.

The poultry sector is, if possible, even more abusive of workers. American plants are moving towards a chain speed of 175 birds per minute. Repetitive injuries are especially rife in poultry processing because some of the work has been replaced with automation, further limiting the range and types of motions required to service the line. Though every major processing company boasts rules and regulations about the right to bathroom breaks, the right to make complaints without retaliation, the right to a safe working environment, adequate medical care and so on, nothing could be further from reality. Report after report from a myriad of advocacy sources in every major poultry-producing country documents exactly the same issues for labour. Wage theft or misrepresentation is rampant through complicated time-card processes to which workers do not have access. Basic rights and safety training are not communicated properly to workers, many of whom do not speak the local language. Injuries and musculoskeletal disorders such as severe carpal tunnel syndrome, 'claw' hands and permanent nerve damage to the upper body are endemic. There is an almost total failure to adequately treat suffering workers with skilled medical personnel. Retaliation in the form of 'points' or suspension or firing for either taking time off for medical issues, or consulting a doctor who is not hired by the parent company, is common. Because the poultry sector is the least unionized of any in the meat industry, these abuses are even less likely to be addressed by management.[8]

There are significant respiratory consequences for workers in meatpacking across the board. The heavy use of chlorine to sanitize equipment and often carcasses causes many workers to develop chronic respiratory diseases, often in spite of wearing respirators. Even in countries where chlorine is not the chemical of choice to sanitize, other compounds can be equally caustic over the course of a worker's shift. Poultry workers are further compromised by feather and poultry litter dust that comes in with the birds. These dangers are simply a cost of doing business for workers, as sanitary requirements demand the use of high-pressure hot water washes and strong chemicals to dissolve the grease and blood, and denature the many pathogens that arrive on the carcasses of the animals. Occupational Safety and Health organizations have regulations and recommendations for mitigating the impact of using these chemicals, but workers cannot escape the damage from working day in and day out in this environment. Many workers report that they receive little to no training on how to use the chemicals required to sanitize a plant or carcass; thus injuries can include skin and eye burns, along with the respiratory issues.

Overall and across the world, the meat industry has demonstrated a callous lack of regard for the labour force that generates its profits. While the European Union 15 (the first 15 countries to join up) offer more protections than many other countries, in the form of stronger labour laws and better enforcement of labour standards, they too are guilty of serious exploitation and abuse of guest or undocumented workers. What drives this aspect of the industry is the tight profit margins inherent in any agricultural enterprise. Land may rise or fall in value. The cost of feed, the biggest variable in meat production, is subject to the vagaries of the market. Transportation costs vary according to energy prices. The value of the actual product can fluctuate enormously as shortages or gluts occur. Labour? That is entirely the purview of the company. Thus the pressure to drive down that fixed cost is relentless.

Constantly training new workers is a small price to pay for all the savings realized by keeping wages down and benefits minimal or non-existent. The same holds true for paying fines that may accrue from issues relating to unfair labour practices. Until the fines become significant impediments to profit, it can be assumed that there will be no reforms. Moreover, without a level playing field in terms of wages and rights worldwide the downward spiral of conditions for labour in meatpacking will continue unabated. As the meat industry grows, the need for government intervention would seem ever more urgent. Even in countries where labour law has been well established, the abuses that are documented so broadly speak to the difficulty of monitoring practices and enforcing basic protections. In countries where the industry is expanding, such as in South America and Asia, it is hard to see how labour issues will be addressed in a meaningful way any time soon.

7
CONCENTRATION AND CONSOLIDATION IN THE INDUSTRY

Over the last fifty years, the meat industry has reshaped itself from a wide variety of small farms supplying multiple regional processing plants, to a handful of companies operating just a few large packing plants. In many ways this consolidation has been the source of the incredibly cheap meat supply worldwide. It isn't hard to see how that would come about. Larger plants offer economies of scale impossible for smaller plants to achieve. When the cost per unit comes down, that saving is reflected in prices for the consumer. Consumption patterns have changed too. Poultry, once a Sunday supper ritual, is now the world's most consumed protein. Consumption of beef has declined and pork has remained fairly flat – no big fluctuations there, despite the unquenchable appetite for bacon. Now that virtually everyone has access to some form of cheap animal protein, it's worth taking a look at how industry changes have brought us that decadent option at every meal.

Concentration and consolidation are the gospel and creed of the meat industry. Concentration has occurred in the form of one firm gobbling up another, acquiring its processing plants and supply chains. To give an idea of what that means, independent pork producers have diminished by 70 per cent in the last twenty years in the United States. Eighty per cent of all beef slaughtered in the USA is concentrated in four companies.[1] The trend towards larger slaughterhouses is being adopted across Europe, albeit at a slower pace than that seen in Australia, South America and the USA. This difference is likely due to regional tastes, and the different ways in which meat is cut and further processed in the member countries of the EU. But as Brazilian and American companies seek to acquire more European companies and facilities, it isn't hard to anticipate the model changing in the EU.

Around the world, companies are briskly buying and selling different aspects of the meat supply chain. Whether it is expanding from beef into pork and poultry, or expansion into 'added value' products such as batter-coated nuggets à la McDonald's, sausages, beef patties or bacon, no major meat industry player stays in just one category these days. It's crucial to have 'horizontal integration' as a business model. Beef consumption goes down, chicken goes up. Who wants to be stuck with nothing but cattle? Not JBS, Cargill or Tyson. These companies have bought up and down the food chain. It isn't just about 'horizontal integration' either. The real moneymaker is what is called 'vertical integration'.

To understand what an incredibly smart concept vertical integration is, we must pay homage to the poultry industry, and especially Don Tyson. Though Tyson was by no means the first poultry grower to figure out how profitable a contract model of livestock production would be, he must be credited with the astonishing success in standardizing and expanding it.

Here is how it works. The company – say, Tyson, since they invented this – produces the feed in its own feedmills. They identify and produce the genetics of their birds. They incubate and hatch millions of eggs. They control all the vaccinations or medicines needed to raise healthy birds. They have their own veterinarians who oversee the well-being of the flocks. Lastly, they own the processing piece, including any added-value processing beyond just cutting birds up for grocery stores or other institutional buyers. They own the trucks in which all of these components make their way from one part of the process to the next. In other words, the company controls literally every aspect of the supply chain, from food and medicine, to egg and chick, to parts and nuggets. However, there is another player in the scheme: the grower.

The 'grower' owns the facility in which the birds 'grow out', typically a very large barn, housing as many as 20,000 birds, or even up to 50,000, as you might find in Brazil. Most growers have at least two or three houses. The company will sign a contract with a grower that says they will supply day-old chicks, and the grower agrees to raise them with the oversight and input of the company. Once a flock achieves slaughter weight, the company comes to pick up the birds, and delivers another flock of chicks to the grower.

The grower is paid for the weight of the birds at the end of the grow-out phase, minus the cost of the feed supplied by the company. His success in growing out the birds to maximum weight in minimal time and with minimal mortality is what guarantees his profit. The chief benefit to the grower is that the company provides a dependable market for the birds. No worries about where or how he will sell 20,000 chickens at a clip. The company takes care of that, along with their transportation. However, the grower is also responsible for any mortality, meaning that if chickens die, he owns them. The grower pays for the utilities in his chicken house. Given the need to maintain a median temperature and the all-important ventilation necessary to keep poultry alive in the miasma of noxious gases arising from thousands of animals defecating, that can be a fairly hefty price.

The integrator, or parent company, may or may not contribute to the cost of the 'litter' on the floor of the barns where the chickens live. This can be a combination of wood shavings, rice hulls, sand or any other type of substrate necessary to absorb the faeces, dust, spilled feed and water that accrues from all the animals. The grower pays for any employees needed to help manage the facility. The grower owns the 'litter', the disposal of which is his problem as well. In the poultry industry, the amount varies between 120 and 150 tons per year per house.[2] Poultry litter is used as fertilizer and in some cases as a supplement to cattle feed. The feathers are considered protein. It's not clear what role the faecal matter plays in nutrition. Litter destined for feed is processed to remove pathogens and presumably drug residues, thus giving growers another place to go with the massive quantities of waste product that emanate from a poultry house. All in all, this type of integration allows for the incredibly cheap prices for chicken that are seen across the industry.

So you might wonder: where are the downsides? Well, some of the downsides have to do with how the contracts between integrator and grower are managed and distributed, including price per pound, as well as the genetics and general health of the chicks. As Christopher Leonard explains at length in his seminal exposé of the poultry industry, *The Meat Racket*, integrators don't always have to reveal price per pound until the birds are grown and weighed. If a grower should get a flock of chicks of lesser quality, they may not gain weight well, or they may die in large numbers. The mortality of the birds will have a potentially disastrous impact on his or her profit margin, and many growers complain of unfair practices on the part of the integrator in how birds are allocated. The grower can be graded by the integrator without knowing what those ratings look like, or why they received them. The ratings can have an impact on the awarding of future contracts. As Leonard explains it, the growers are pitted against one another in what are called Tournaments, a term emphatically denied by the poultry industry. Instead they describe it as 'a performance-based structure that aligns with fundamental free market principles to encourage efficiency and improve performance'.[3] There seems to be a significant cadre of growers who would dispute that description; however, the industry flatly denies that there might be something unfair about creating an environment where growers are forced to compete with one another in order to guarantee the flow of contracts essential to their economic survival.

Then there are start-up costs for joining an integrator as a grower. Typically the grower has to take out significant loans to build the poultry houses and equip them. The loss of part or all of a flock will not only jeopardize the contract and future contracts with the integrator, but the possibility of property loss when loans are unpaid is very real and a frequent cause of financial ruin. The integrator can also demand improvements or changes in the chicken house in order for the grower to be awarded another contract. This might necessitate more loans. In short, the system is stacked against the growers, who absorb all the risk while the integrators reap the profits. This system of vertical integration has now been heavily replicated in the pork industry in the United States and elsewhere, with similar outcomes, both in terms of profitability for the integrator and abuses of the growers who have few options available to recoup from losses. They have even fewer options when it comes to finding an independent abattoir should they elect to strike out on their own.

Contract poultry farming is now the industry norm, no matter where it is practised. Because the poultry industry is relatively new in the sense of the volume it now commands, it has been easier to start growers off in this direction rather than attempting to change an industry already entrenched in long-time practices. The cattle industry does not lend itself in quite the same way to a contract model, but the pork industry does. Over the last twenty years alone, the number of hog farmers in the USA has declined from over 590,000 in 1981 (typically small or medium-sized integrated farms) to under 30,000, many of whom are contract growers for major pork-producing companies.[4] The Tyson model essentially created the vertical integration that characterizes pork and poultry production today in most countries.

Looking beyond the grower's experience, vertical integration can forever alter the nature of a town or county. Prior to the evolution of the contract system, livestock production could support an entire community. There might be multiple farmers growing the grain and a few different feedmills for processing it. There might be multiple sources for chicks because there are plenty of farmers selling them, and, incidentally, maintaining hybrid vigour. There would be a local processing plant that would employ more people. Truckers would make a living hauling grain to and from farms, as well as the finished products to future buyers. All in all, the town or county would support a pretty broad swathe of agricultural production with a slot for most residents somewhere along the supply chain. Vertical integration has put a halt to all that. With only one company centrally owning all the elements in the chain, there are far fewer opportunities for people to find work in their locale. This one factor can explain a lot about why rural communities have seen so much of their populations relocate to more urban areas.

Whereas pork and poultry processing is almost completely in the hands of the parent company or integrator, the cattle sector operates quite differently. Cattle go through three stages and each one is presided over by a different type of operator. They start with cow/calf, where females are bred and calves are born and raised to a certain weight. Once they reach that weight milestone, they might go off to a feeder/stocker, step two on the path to steaks and chops. Most often these two stages are on pasture, or a mix of pasture and fodder depending on the location and season. Step three is the finisher/feedlot. This is what most people associate with the raising of cattle, where they are confined and fed grain.

Grain is expensive compared to grass, so the actual time in the feedlot is generally no more than a few months at most. The feedlot owner is the one who sells to the packing plant and it is here that the price really gets beaten down, a result that has an impact on the whole chain going backwards. In cattle-producing countries around the world, the people who run the cattle are hamstrung by lack of options because of the lack of competition among processors. If JBS operates the only plant within 1,000 miles of a ranch, then that is the plant that will process those animals. The option to move animals farther not only begs the welfare question, but has a serious impact on slaughter weight as the stress and lack of feed during the journey cause cattle to shed weight.

If a farmer or rancher is operating independently, that is, without long-standing ties to one or more processors, finding a place to go with their animals is challenging. Once processed, the farmer is then obliged to locate the markets in which to sell their beef, rather than the typical scenario where the packer buys the beef and funnels it into their integrated supply chain of grocery stores, restaurants or further processing, all controlled by that packing company. For smaller farms or ranches with a string of farmers' markets, or a local wholesale distributor to work with, selling product is manageable. If a medium- to large-size rancher opts out of the mainstream of industry the difficulties of moving, storing and selling the product become nearly insurmountable. Woe to the producer who complains about the price, or how the animal was graded. Next time they are ready to bring animals to slaughter, they may find themselves unable to get an appointment, or they may confront even lower prices. Every extra day a cow is on feed costs that producer any profit they may squeeze out of raising beef.

In the early days of the industry, the consolidation of meatpackers was bucked by the Packers and Stockyards Act of 1921. By the 1920s, only five companies (Armour, Cudahy, Morris, Swift and Wilson) controlled the prices and the processing of virtually all pork and beef in the United States. Recognizing the impact that was having on farmers and ranchers, the Act successfully reined in the price-fixing and monopolies perpetrated by the 'Big Five' and meat processing proceeded on a more equitable basis for all. Until now. Currently, 80 per cent of all the pork and beef processing in the USA is done by one of the major four processors: JBS, Tyson, Cargill and National Beef.[5]

While the USA and Brazil have the most concentration, and the fewest processing options for the average farmer, the EU is undergoing its own transformation. The UK once had 600–700 poultry companies, just thirty years ago. That number is now down to six large companies, which contract with farmers just as they do in the USA and elsewhere.[6] As competition between the big integrators ratchets up, the likelihood of further consolidation, from larger companies buying up the smaller, seems all but certain.

With minimum wages much higher than in other countries, Denmark, the Netherlands, France, the UK and others are caught in a bind that they are solving by exporting their processing to other EU countries with lower labour costs, such as Poland or Germany, which relies heavily on labour contractors who bring in lower-wage foreign workers. Denmark, the biggest pork producer in the EU, has built its own plants in Germany in order to cash in on more relaxed labour laws and cheaper workers. European meat companies are competitively disadvantaged in multiple ways. They have higher labour costs in general than other regions. They have much stricter environmental controls, a factor that tightens their margins even further. They are more dependent on imported feed for their poultry and pork, with fluctuating costs. Finally, despite having traditionally shielded their industry from lower-cost meat by using tariff protections, these are being eroded through new trade deals. European processors also suffer from under-production. They don't always have the enormous supply in the pipeline that is necessary to profitable operations. All of these factors will contribute to further consolidation in their region.

Brazil appears to have actually encouraged monopolies. In the race to become internationally competitive, internal competition was a casualty.[7] However, legislation passed in 2013 has made the types of mergers and acquisitions so damaging to competition much more difficult to effect. Nevertheless, by the time that legislation passed, the industry had already consolidated into four major companies; JBS, BRF, Minerva and Marfrig. The four had acquired so many smaller Brazilian companies that the government regulatory body, CADE, was obliged to step in. Since then, those companies have been trading in U.S. and European meat businesses, buying up either divisions or whole firms in a race to dominate the world market for animal proteins. Though Brazil suffered from foot-and-mouth disease, which significantly limited its export market for beef, new markets in China have given it back its edge. Truly Brazil has emerged as a crushing force in the meat industry, with subsidiaries and operations all over the world. It represents the leading competition to every other major production centre on the planet.

The undue influence of consolidation on producers can be seen especially clearly in Australia, where running cattle (and sheep) occupy an historic place in agriculture. There are still thousands of producers growing animals out on their 'stations'. What has changed is the number of plants where they can bring their animals for slaughter. This is where that bottleneck really shows up. In the 1970s there were five hundred plants just for export trade. Nowadays the number is more like sixty.[8] With a lack of competition in processing, producers are obliged to take what they can get in terms of price per pound. This echoes the scenario in the United States and Brazil, where packers control the supply chain in ways that dramatically reduce the profitability of cattle producers. The Australian 'red meat' sector is fighting back. In hearings before the Australian Senate they have made demands that the government intercede by demanding more transparency in pricing, with some sort of baseline guarantee when a producer hands his or her herd over to the processor.[9]

If a dozen companies wind up owning all the processing of the world's meat supply it seems reasonable to expect the usual results from a monopoly: loss of quality and increased price-fixing. It's a bit of a mystery why antitrust laws are not coming into play in the USA at least, where just four packers essentially own the industry. While Brazil may have a new interest in protecting against monopolies, the cow, as it were, is out of the barn there. Asia is inviting in American and Brazilian companies to set up their industrial model. The EU is struggling to maintain its independent farmers, but without plenty of local abattoirs to support them they are likely to fall victim to the same fate. Australians are protesting at the stranglehold meatpackers have on their farmers and ranchers. There seems to be little interest on the part of governments in reining in the inexorable advance of multinational meatpackers. As the packers get bigger, the power concentrated in their hands grows exponentially, and that will have unforeseen and probably terrible impacts on rural communities, farming and agriculture throughout the world.

8
FOOD FRAUD

Food fraud is a collective term that encompasses the deliberate and intentional substitution, addition, tampering or misrepresentation of food, food ingredients or food packaging; or false or misleading statements made about a product for economic gain. Our research has not expanded into misbranding or marketing fraud where a producer overstates performance attributes or violates 'truth in advertising' laws or 'country of origin' claims.

Doug Moyer, Michigan State University, Food Fraud Initiative

Food travels far and fast these days. Most developed countries source their daily food from all over the world thanks to that miracle known as a grocery store. Aisles are full of fruits and vegetables that have no business being there out of season. Spices we had never heard of a decade ago have proliferated. The expansion of the 'international' aisle is a testament to the impact of food shows on television along with restaurants showing off every possible cuisine. Accompanying the bounty of products, there is a bounty of food fraud to match. In fact, it is a very big business, estimated at up to U.S.$40 billion a year.[1]

The usual fraudulent suspects are olive oil, honey, spices, teas, coffees and fish. That pricey green ooze from Italy or Spain might well be peanut oil with food colouring and some chemical aromatics, or worse. Spices can be loaded with brick dust or industrial dye. Teas can just be a handful of dried leaves off someone's backyard shrub in a fancy package. Ground coffee? Twigs, corn, wheat chaff.

And then, of course, there is meat. People buy a lot of prepared foods nowadays. Anything that comes in a package from a freezer and is not a whole muscle cut like a steak or a chop is a candidate for food fraud. Think how easy, how tempting, it would be to add some filler to ground (minced) beef patties, or into a meat pie or lasagne. For the manufacturer, it could potentially save thousands from their costs. How would anyone know, when so many of those products are pumped full of flavouring agents or, once cooked, smothered with ketchup, mustard or mayo? Pretty hard to tell if that product is 100 per cent of anything, right?

This very scenario played out in the UK in 2013. In a series of random tests conducted by the Food Safety Authority of Ireland, some ground beef patties were discovered to contain not just beef, but horsemeat and a smidgen of pork. An investigation quickly followed and it was discovered that a major supplier to the supermarket Tesco had purchased meat from another supplier who had bought cheap meat from Poland and added it into the patties. The patties were destined for the bargain aisle at Tesco stores.

More investigations ensued and more products were found to contain varying degrees of horsemeat, right up to 100 per cent of the product being sold. In that particular case, it was a popular ready-to-eat lasagne and a Bolognese sauce. Those products came from different suppliers in a variety of countries. It soon became clear that these adulterated products were not just the province of Tesco, Aldi, ASDA, Lidl or the Dunnes Stores. This was a much wider problem. Major institutional caterers such as Sodexo, a supplier to schools and universities, found horsemeat in their products. Birds Eye Foods found horsemeat in their chilli con carne in Belgium, the meat sold to them by a Belgian firm. Burger King dropped their UK supplier when they discovered horsemeat in their Whoppers!

Over the next few months, from December 2012, when the first samples were discovered, to January 2013, when the scandal broke in the press, and on through February of that year, country after country discovered that they, too, had a horsemeat problem. Eventually it came to light that one particular firm, with tentacles deep in the supply chain, had been purchasing horsemeat from Romania, relabelling it as ground beef and selling it to a swathe of manufacturers. Another batch of horse-tainted ground meat came from the Netherlands. Altogether, eight major food suppliers withdrew products containing ground beef due to the presence of horse DNA in their samples. One large hotel company was indicted for concealing the presence of horsemeat in their food. Though the offending supplier swore they were the ones who had been hoodwinked, some felt this was a case of déjà vu. One of the players from that same supplier had been convicted six years before for selling horsemeat labelled as beef.

Horsemeat turned up in products in the Netherlands, Spain, France and Sweden as well as the UK. The sources were as varied as West Yorkshire, Wales, France, Romania, Poland and the Netherlands, and possibly even the USA via

Mexico. Thanks to the Rapid Alert System for Food and Feed already in place, the UK was able to pursue the investigation as well as alert other member countries about the adulteration of the food supply. Sometimes the chain was easy to follow, other times impossible. What was clear, however, was that the movement of food between EU members was largely uninspected, untested and often untraceable. Obviously something major had to be done. Emergency meetings were scheduled in Brussels with food safety authorities from a number of countries. They drafted a long memo detailing the many flaws of the food safety and inspection services within the EU, among them: 'no statistics exist on the incidence of food fraud in the EU, and . . . the Commission has only recently identified food fraud as a new area of action . . .', and this one: 'the massive-scale fraud of horsemeat meals throughout Europe is the symptom of an uncontrollable globalised supply system, cut-price agri-food productivism and an incomplete labeling system . . .'[2] That last statement lays bare the problems facing every country engaged in importing or exporting food products.

The memo also contained some valuable definitions of food fraud, which is certainly not limited to exchanging or substituting one ingredient for another. Standard definitions of food fraud remain largely absent in the EU, so harmonizing them was considered key to pursuing better enforcement of existing regulations, along with developing new ones. The last part of the memo included a great number of recommendations regarding how to police food more effectively, how to hold suppliers more accountable, how to maintain traceability between countries, new testing procedures, and many more. Suffice it to say that there were so many recommendations for improving the system that it is clear that there was, in fact, no system at all.

This remarkable story – remarkable for the convoluted nature of the supply chain of processed foods – played out in the UK tabloids for several months. It was, obviously, a major embarrassment to the supermarkets and grocery chains that had been selling these products. A store chain or a brand is only as good as its reputation, and clearly this scandal had major repercussions on their bottom lines. Demands for retooling the supply chain and purchasing processes were made, and editorials were published on how the UK government had let down the public by enacting major budget cuts in the organizations responsible for food testing and safety. The number of inspectors had, in fact, recently been cut savagely, and the meat industry was apparently policing itself, or so it was alleged in several publications.[3] It has never been clear just how long this horsemeat scam had been going on, but a cynical mind might conclude that the discovery in December 2012 just scratched the surface of what may well have been months if not years of substitution and adulteration.

The reality is that with the complex nature of how processed foods are made, it is devilishly difficult to monitor every last stop along the way of the chain. Furthermore, in the anti-regulatory atmosphere that dominates many of today's governments, the same budget cuts that contributed to the failures in the horsemeat scandal are being enacted in other countries. The average consumer would consider it necessary for regular and consistent testing and inspection to be mandatory. Not so for grocery store chains, meat companies and a host of other food producers who manipulate labels, ingredients and data in highly ingenious ways to improve their margins. These entities lobby governments intensely to 'back off' from bothersome and 'redundant' regulations or processes that are inconvenient to producers.

Labelling is a perfect example of how the public is duped through language. The word 'natural' is emblematic for 'greenwashing' a product, no matter what it is. Tell a consumer that something is 'natural' and their mind will frequently entertain visions of a bucolic meadow dotted with wild flowers and frolicking animals. Or they may think of fields of undulating grains, grown with nothing more than gentle rain and golden rays of sunshine. How about dairy products? Immaculate eggs, coyly peeping out from under the happy mummy hen; buckets of creamy milk, just stripped from the teat by a rosy-cheeked milkmaid. It's almost too much fun to even think of this stuff, and, indeed, marketing companies are paid millions to create and successfully project these wholly inaccurate images to the consumer. The reality is that 'natural' means absolutely nothing in a legal, 'labelly' sort of way. So though it is not illegal to use that word as a descriptive on a label, it is certainly misleading. When meat is labelled 'natural', it doesn't mean that the animal grew up on pasture, or that its feed was organic, or that it received no vaccines, hormones or growth promotants. It merely means that it has no artificial ingredients and that it is 'minimally processed'. Is that actually fraud?

No, but it speaks to an attitude within the food system that sees confusing and misleading the public about the quality of their food as perfectly legitimate. It's not hard to see how that attitude in suppliers can lead to something like the horsemeat scandal in the EU. The unfolding of that story illustrated vividly how each step along the supply chain blamed the one before, claiming to have no knowledge, or inkling, that anything might be amiss. Maybe that is true. Maybe it is not. The end result was a miserable failure to protect the public from unscrupulous purveyors who took advantage of the opacity of the supply chain to make millions in profit.

Labelling can also be directly falsified. Many grocery stores have been found guilty of changing sell-by labels on anything from meat to cake. That particular scam can include further adulteration, such as re-grinding old meat with a small amount of fresh to improve the colour. Giving meat a chlorine rinse to diminish a funky smell is another tactic. The practice of 'adding water' is ubiquitous. In this particular con, meat is soaked in a saline solution or water is simply injected into the meat. This is perfectly legal, by the way – as long as the added water remains under a certain limit – and is widely practised. Obviously, since most meat is sold by weight, this will add precious grams to the price tag while costing the producer nothing. The opportunities in this arena are incalculable.

Nowadays products are labelled as 'fair trade', 'organic', 'free range', 'halal', 'certified humane' and a host of other assurances that what a consumer buys squares with their values. Though certainly most companies making those claims are honest, there is virtually no mechanism that can assure they are compliant with the definitions of those words.

Indeed, the harmonization of those definitions has yet to be implemented, so one country's 'fair trade' could mean something completely different in another country.

Every country with a functioning food system is dealing with the issues of food fraud. Consider the Chinese and the horrific scandal of melamine, a plastic, substituted for powdered milk in baby formula. Or the more humorous but no less offensive incident of the 'five spice' donkey snacks popular in northern China found to be made of fox. To a Western eye, neither donkey nor fox is appetizing, but, worse, we also cannot say that fox is safe to eat. As with the dangers of consuming 'bushmeat' in Africa, a fox may have any number of scary pathogens that could lead to significant illness or death. The Chinese have also found rat and mink being sold as beef. With the new-found interest in eating meat, corrupt individuals are capitalizing on a public appetite that seems coupled with a relatively untutored palate, unable to distinguish beef, pork or chicken from other species. (It should be noted, though, that rat meat is eaten quite openly in Vietnam, and skinned, eviscerated rats are sold in many of the southern markets.)

Substitutions and additions are rampant in the meat supply. Australia found that its 'lamb' was often mutton. Mutton is much cheaper, so labelling it as lamb made for a tidy uptick in profit. Ground veal is often chicken. Meat labelled halal might be anything but. Pork is a frequent undeclared addition to ground beef, particularly when the price of beef goes up, as it has in the last half-decade.

Since the horsemeat scandal erupted in Europe, every country has become acutely more aware of the multibillion-dollar business of food fraud. By 2014 the EU member states had met numerous times and made progress on a number of fronts to regulate the movement of food between countries. An extensive report was commissioned from Professor Chris Elliott at Queen's University in Belfast. Elliott's work on drug residues and chemical contaminants in agro-industrial products gave him the expertise necessary to lead the review of the UK food system in the wake of 'Horse-gate'. Within a year he had produced a 146-page report identifying 'eight pillars of food integrity'. His report called for the establishment of a Food Crimes Unit, along with strategies for intelligence gathering, information sharing among law enforcement entities domestically and internationally, audits and spot inspections and a host of other sensible recommendations. Whether all of those measures will be implemented depends on how much money each country is willing to spend on protecting its population from food fraud. Not surprisingly, every member country has its own ideas on how to pay and who should be paying. Getting every member on the same wavelength will undoubtedly take some Herculean diplomacy.

The EU does have a major tool for identifying food fraud. In 2013 the Food Fraud Network was created to allow members to exchange information with ease. A variety of dedicated IT tools have been adopted, along with a huge database of incidents and types of food fraud to help countries recognize repeat offenders or how a particular product may fit into a criminal organization's profile. With the huge amount of money involved in food fraud around the world, organized crime, including drug cartels, is often behind specious products. The olive oil industry, for example, suffers greatly from the predations of Italian organized crime.

In newer technological developments, just since 2013, mass spectrometry, a technique for identifying the origins of specific molecules, has been applied to food with some success. DNA fingerprinting has also become more available and is being used extensively, particularly in meat products. A paper published by the Royal Society of Chemistry in 2015 suggests that in the near future, using these and other sophisticated techniques, it may be possible to develop handheld tools that would function as 'point and shoot' devices to be used all along a supply chain.[4] Besides being able to detect fraudulent ingredients, these devices could also revolutionize the identification of bacterial pathogens within the food supply. Contamination of meat and other products from common sources of illness such as *Campylobacter* or *Salmonella* could be detected before the product goes out to market, a major advance in food safety.

Another component to addressing food fraud in the EU has been the application of Country of Origin Labelling (COOL). Traceability in the food supply would seem to be an elementary component of ensuring food integrity. As it is currently formulated, the COOL regulations in the EU have been extended from beef to include pork, poultry, goats and sheep.[5] This new requirement was implemented in 2014, and not surprisingly the meat industry as well as food processors and grocery chains have registered many objections. The mandatory COOL requires that information on where an animal was born, slaughtered and processed is included on the label, and this rule applies to both whole muscle meat and ground meat.

Manufacturers project that mandatory COOL will cost the consumer 15–50 per cent extra, due to the administrative activities in collecting and coordinating this information and then communicating it to the packaging entity. That figure has been heavily disputed and other groups in favour of COOL have proposed that it would cost U.S.1.5 cents per label.[6] There can be no doubt that segregating animals either live or as carcasses, trim or cuts, and then identifying where those animals were born, raised and then slaughtered, is an onerous process. And yet, there is certainly a justifiable argument to be made for it given the global nature of the food supply, and the lack of transparency in how ingredients are acquired and used.

More recently the EU has been considering COOL for processed foods, such as pre-formed beef patties, lasagnes, Bolognese sauce and other products where ground or processed meat of some form is included. This measure would certainly facilitate the trace-back of those types of products in the wake of another adulteration episode such as the horsemeat scandal. Up until 2015 the United States had the same COOL rules as the EU, identifying place of birth, slaughter and processing. However, beginning in 2009 two North American Free Trade Act (NAFTA) partners, Canada and Mexico, filed a case with the WTO stating that COOL acted as a 'barrier to trade', incentivizing consumers to select U.S. products over Canadian or Mexican. Faced with something approaching U.S.$3 billion in fines or retaliatory tariffs for violating trade laws, the U.S. Congress caved in and repealed COOL for beef and pork in May 2015. Labelling for lamb and poultry remains in place. If the Transatlantic Trade and Investment Partnership, currently being negotiated, is passed, it seems plausible that any country within that agreement will object to COOL compliance just as Canada or Mexico did, unless it presents a marketing opportunity.

Country of Origin Labelling is popular with consumers, even if it isn't with the industry. A Consumers Union poll conducted in 2010, and another poll in 2013 by the Consumer Federation of America, showed overwhelmingly that people do want to know where their meat originates. With food fraud as rampant as it is, consumers might well be willing to pay extra to know where the ground meat in their frozen dinner comes from. Food safety standards can be quite disparate among the meat-producing regions. So are standards for animal welfare, labour and environmental concerns. Country of Origin Labelling provides consumers with just about the only tool at their disposal that allows them to vote with their wallets for or against a particular system.

Despite all the drama surrounding the horsemeat scandal and the meetings and reports and even legislative efforts that have been forthcoming, food fraud remains a persistent problem in the EU. A November 2015 report from the BEUC, the EU consumer protection agency, found that mislabelling, added water and adulterated products are endemic.[7] One member claimed that of the many samples collated among the member countries, fully half were found to show examples of one kind of fraud or another. From sausages that only had half the meat they were claimed to contain, to questions about what kind of meat was included, there were serious problems identified with processed and takeaway foods.

In response, the EU commission tasked with the investigation into fraud pointed to the new IT Administrative Assistance and Cooperation System, designed to allow for the rapid exchange of information around fraud, as well as several other EU-funded technological initiatives. The real problem seems to be that some members are more concerned with fraud than others. The EU Commissioner for Safety and Health, Vytenis Andriukaitis, responded to the report with this:

> The enforcement of the Union's food chain rules lies with the Member States, which are required to run a system of official controls to verify that the relevant requirements are fulfilled at all stages of the food chain. They shall take into account any available relevant information that might suggest non-compliance in order to organize their enforcement activities and better target their controls.[8]

So much for cooperation in the EU. Until and unless each member country allocates funds and personnel to test, audit and report on incidents of food fraud, it is unlikely to abate any time soon.

As we have seen, food fraud is everywhere, including the United States. Figures on food fraud concerning meat are not available, but the seafood industry has been heavily scrutinized. A 2013 study on seafood in the USA, conducted by the non-profit organization Oceana, identified up to 35 per cent of the samples they tested as either mislabelled or not containing fish. With specific popular species such as tuna or salmon, the level of deception exceeded 59 per cent of the samples. Fish that is processed and frozen in the form of fish fillets, or fish fingers, is very difficult to identify. A fish that is labelled as grey sole, for instance, could be any number of white-fleshed fish with a similar shape. The difference in cost of grey sole vs a doppelganger can be quite significant, however, and that is where the profit margin soars. Similar to the meat industry, the number of inspectors looking at and testing fish has been subjected to many of the same budget cuts that incidentally benefit large companies by allowing them to police themselves.

With food fraud so common among trading partners, it is curious that no one seems to have subjected the American meat supply to the same rigorous inspection, despite the fact that the country is a net importer of beef, pork and lamb.[9] As a nation with few home cooks, the use of prepared and processed foods is ubiquitous, inviting the question: why has there been no large-scale ongoing examination of the meat industry for fraud involving substitution, mislabelling and adulteration? Undoubtedly the reason can be found in the ever-tightening budgets offered to regulatory agencies such as the USDA Food Safety and Inspection Services and the FDA. These agencies are charged with monitoring the food supply for the USA, and up to now the focus has been on food safety far more than food fraud, notwithstanding the events in Europe in 2013. With food-borne illness rampant, the principal task for the agencies has been to identify contaminated meat, dairy and produce. In reality, the agencies are unable to inspect more than 2.3 per cent of all the foods imported into the USA, including meat.[10]

One might also speculate on the power of the meat lobby in determining whether or not the industry is subjected to the same scrutiny as the seafood industry. Given that much of the meat imported into the USA winds up in ground meat, it would seem logical that substitutions could be easily inserted into the supply chain with no one the wiser. As it stands, processing plants test only for pathogens that cause food-borne illness. No evidence has come to light indicating that the actual DNA is being regularly examined to be sure that what is supposed to be beef, pork or lamb is in fact those species.[11] In a fairly recent test conducted at Chapman University in California, 48 samples of ground meat were tested using DNA and other techniques, and ten of those were found to be contaminated with other meats. Two contained horsemeat. One sample could not even be identified.[12] Despite that somewhat disturbing proportion of positive samples for adulterated ground meat, no alarm bells have been rung stateside. It should also be noted that horse abattoirs were abolished in the USA in 2006, and horsemeat banned from sale. Horses from the USA that are not pets are shipped to Mexico or Canada for processing. What's to stop a dodgy processor from wringing a little more profit from a trading partner?

In spite of the minimal inspection of meat for fraud, the USA has several excellent tools to identify it. One of them is the relatively newly created Food Fraud Initiative at Michigan State University. As part of the Food Safety Modernization Act signed into law by President Barack Obama in 2011, the Food Fraud Initiative works with industry and across disciplines sharing research and studies, as well as offering courses and webinars that are open to everyone. The group is also affiliated with an international cohort of academics and scientists who are working to reduce the vulnerabilities of our global food chain.

Another arrow in the quiver is a non-profit organization called the U.S. Pharmacopeial Convention, or USP. Though it was established primarily for medical purposes, it includes food ingredients in its database. The standards set by the USP are accepted in 140 countries.[13] The USP documents and analyses food additives and chemical ingredients common to the food supply. With so many processed foods now on the market, and the potential for additives being substituted or adulterated, this database is an invaluable tool in identifying fraud.

The best way to combat food fraud seems to be to buy as little processed or prepared food as possible, and to purchase from known or branded sources. A company that has made its reputation for being reliable and honest will be the company most committed to maintaining a safe and traceable food supply, no matter what the ingredient is. When a consumer is tempted to purchase a product at an abnormally low price, they should question why that price is so low. Sometimes a deal really is too good to be true.

9
TRADE DEALS AND LAND GRABS

As the meat industry has consolidated, a key trend in acquisitions has emerged. Where once a large company would buy up a smaller one within the same nation, now we increasingly see that huge corporations are purchasing assets in other countries in order to expand their growth into foreign markets, sometimes without even having to build or staff a new outlet. The most famous example of this was the sale in 2013 of Smithfield, America's largest pork company, to Shuanghui, a Chinese company, now owned by WH Group. Combined with its Chinese counterparts, this multinational conglomerate is now the world's largest producer and processor of pork. Smithfield alone employs 48,000 people worldwide, with facilities concentrated in the southeast of the USA and in Poland and Romania. What made this sale so exceptional was not the potential for an antitrust suit (for which it should have been eligible long before the acquisition), but the unprecedented transfer of agricultural assets from one country to another. While JBS has absorbed major beef packers in the USA and Australia, the animals and feed remain at least partly owned by the host country. In the case of the Smithfield sale to Shuanghui, no other deal to date has included a supply chain as complete.

Consider this: Smithfield owns some 26 facilities in the USA, including the largest pork-processing facility in the world. It owns breeding sows and boars, weanlings, feeders and finished pigs. It also owns the slaughterhouses, feed mills and added-value processing companies that turn their pigs into bacon, sausages and hams, along with fresh pork. Smithfield owns the land on which the crops that feed its pigs are grown. It obviously uses vast quantities of water to irrigate, to feed the pigs, for waste management, and then for processing and cleaning. This may sound repetitive, since we have already discussed the impact of consolidation, but there is a reason to hold this up to the light.

In selling Smithfield to a foreign country, the USA has also sold American water, and American soil for crops. The Chinese now own the facilities, the land, the water, the pigs and the processing. America owns the shit. America owns the methane, the greenhouse gases, the VOCs, the nitrates and the phosphorus. What they don't own is the food supply and the profits. It's a pretty neat deal for the Chinese. Even more troubling about this deal is that the WH Group ties to the Chinese government guarantee that the decisions about company policy will be dictated by a sovereign nation whose foremost concern is the feeding of its population. It also suggests the possibility that, as the largest pork producer in the world, it can manipulate prices for grain and for pork. The need for food in China could mean that it exports every molecule of the pork in the Smithfield supply chain. That would have quite an impact on prices and food security in the USA. For many reasons, the acquisition of farm assets by a foreign government with an appetite like that of the

Chinese is a decidedly risky proposition and one that should be viewed with great scepticism by other nations.

This pattern is being repeated in endless variations around the world. As climate change and water shortages affect the ability to grow food, many countries are already hedging their bets by buying or leasing vast tracts of arable land, or acquiring entire companies like Smithfield. For example, JBS SA is buying companies as fast as it can, including the entire pork division of Cargill USA, and Moy Park, a major British producer of pork. In 2014 they bought the Primo Group, a processed foods company in Australia, as well as Big Frango, a Brazilian company.

In another development, since 2008, when the stock market crashed and food commodities escalated in price, land and agricultural assets have become very attractive targets for banks, hedge funds, pension funds and institutional investors of every stripe. In many cases the investor will manage a company or tract of land, but just as frequently the land is simply held as an investment with the assumption that land values will continue to rise as the need to grow more food escalates.

Certainly the acquiring company is expected to follow the local rules about environment and labour, animal welfare and food safety. The risk is over the long game. Leasing and selling agricultural assets in an era when food security is just beginning to emerge as one of the biggest issues of the twenty-first century seems reckless at best. The distribution of agricultural land and resources to foreign companies can be highly lucrative to the few who manage to capitalize on those deals. If, however, you are a low-income agrarian type, you have just been taken to the cleaners. Your land will be turned over to producing soy, palm oil, sugar, biofuels or meat. The crops needed for you to survive will no longer have a place to grow. Right now the epicentre of these massive acquisitions are Southeast Asia and Africa. Land in South American countries is also a major target for resource-poor nations with a lot of capital to invest in commodities.

In a 2013 report, Oxfam stated that sales of arable land for the use of other regions such as China, the Middle East and North and South America have frequently resulted in increased hunger and poverty in the exploited regions. For example, if China rents or buys 100,000 hectares of land on which to grow and harvest feed for its pigs and chickens, where are locals expected to plant their own food? Consider sub-Saharan countries where not only is the land used for something other than growing food for the population, but the scarce supplies of water are being sucked dry for those crops, and not by the people who need them to wash, bathe and drink, as well as farm. The Oxfam report also noted that the practice of land grabs 'exacerbates social inequality and conflict and worsens the country's existing problem of concentrated land ownership'.[1]

Another facet to this story is the role that banks play in these investments. Australia, for example, is cited in the aforementioned Oxfam report for the failure of its four major banks to conduct due diligence on the companies they loan to or invest in who are working in foreign countries. Many of the projects instigated by multinational food companies fail miserably at providing the jobs or projects promised as a part of the deal. Frequently a company will bring in its own workers, rather than use local labour. Numerous studies have shown that a foreign company will negotiate with a corrupt government anxious to make its own buck, leaving local populations defenceless against the corporation. In the case of four major banks in Australia, the Oxfam report showed that they loaned enormous sums to companies engaged in all kinds of enterprises that included dubious environmental and social impacts. No follow-up reporting was done by the loaning bodies. They apparently took at face value the plans of the borrowing entity to provide goods, jobs, services, infrastructure and so forth to the region they planned to develop. As it turned out, none of those worthy goals was realized. To the contrary, land was damaged, water polluted and local populations displaced, and hunger and poverty escalated. Was this the goal of the good people in Australia who banked with those loaning institutions?[2]

It isn't just loans going into the business of arable land. Investors are using pension funds as well to return a profit in agriculture. This would seem a questionable investment strategy given the volatility of the agricultural sector with the wild card of climate change thrown into the mix. Moreover these retirement funds are being gambled on land investments in countries where the rules of ownership are not clearly defined or upheld. Nonetheless, buying or leasing landholdings is a popular and presently winning strategy for many large institutional investors. TIAA-Cref, a major investor whose portfolio includes many pension funds, was tagged in the *New York Times* for a land grab in Brazil in 2015.[3] Though Brazil and other countries are now taking measures against foreign intervention in landholdings, the rules that exclude foreign investment are easily evaded through a variety of ruses. In this case, TIAA-Cref got into bed with a Brazilian firm that has been amassing land by dealing with a well-known and thoroughly shady character with a reputation for faking land titles, torching crops and intimidating local populations, forcing them to sign over land. The case is still being disputed in the court system. TIAA-Cref claims no knowledge of any of this, and points the finger at the Brazilian partner as the offending party doing business with criminals.

Given the complexity of these deals, and the convoluted legal system in foreign countries, particularly around land acquisition, TIAA-Cref may well be squeaky clean, at least on paper. What this anecdote illustrates, however, is that no matter how committed a company may be to fairness and transparency, there is no substitute for digging deep to establish legal titles and ownership. Should a country like Brazil decide that the land was stolen from the indigenous population, and repatriates it, where does that leave the investor? TIAA-Cref is a company that famously signed on to international principles governing the acquisition of foreign soil, and yet it finds itself in this dubious position.

The Smithfield sale to Shuanghui also presented an alarming trend in how the meat industry is evolving away from the control of the actual producers and packers and into the purview of high finance. Shuanghui International owned Shuanghui Development, the entity that made the purchase (the hammer price was U.S.$4.7 billion). Shuanghui International at that time was mostly controlled by Western money from the Rockefellers, The Carey Group and Goldman Sachs. Shortly after the sale was completed, allowing those financial entities to extract their investment, Shuanghui renamed itself the WH Group and listed itself on the Hong Kong stock exchange, where, it could be assumed, other equity firms would take positions. In and of itself, that would appear to be business as usual. In the case of a company that controls one of the world's largest pork supplies and its ancillary businesses, what it implies is that fundamental decisions about the food supply are being made by financial investors looking to make money for shareholders. The reality is that most investment firms are sadly lacking in information about the key issues that plague intensive livestock production, so broad public concerns, such as food security and public and environmental health, are rarely factored into their bottom line.

Trade deals

Ever since the 1990s, trade agreements and treaties have worked to eliminate tariffs and enhance the role of international trade in all goods. In the current climate of emphasis on 'free trade', a frenzy of major trade treaties is being negotiated around the world. From the Pacific Rim to the EU, every country is jockeying for ever more favourable terms that allow the free flow of goods between nations. In theory this is supposed to benefit everyone involved: more demand equals more trade equals more money. Since not all countries work from the same playbook it's hard to see how that is going to pan out for countries that follow labour laws or environmental regulations. Given that these agreements are negotiated in secret, how the implementation of workers' rights or pollution controls will be rolled out, just to name two major elements, is murky at best. Farmers and ranchers in smaller countries are especially vulnerable to the economies of scale that are available to nations like the USA, Australia and South American countries where there is an ample supply of land to grow feed and livestock. It should also be noted that trade agreements frequently include language that essentially gives a foreign body more rights than that of the domestic governing body. As an example, a trade agreement may say that a local government cannot take legal measures against a foreign investor who fails to make good on promises, or who damages land or communities. The agreement may allow investors rights in development or acquisition that have a negative impact on local populations.[4] Indeed governments can find themselves in an international courtroom if the foreign investor feels some portion of their deal has soured.

Another aspect of the proliferation of liberalized trade is that holding grain supplies as a cushion against spiking prices or genuine shortages has become a strategy of the past. For countries that are net food importers, such as in the Middle East, the loss of control over how products are priced, due to speculation in the commodities market, was a root cause of the food riots of 2007 and 2008. Commodities such as wheat, rice and other staples soared in price, not because of a shortage, but because they could. This in turn encouraged those Middle Eastern countries to seek to acquire land and leases of their own to avoid a repetition of the cycle.

With a fascinating tool called the Land Matrix, it is possible to map who is buying where, how much land they are buying and for what purpose. It is not completely accurate, by its own admission, because deals are struck or abandoned daily. Nevertheless the data is absolutely stunning. Rumours swirl around how much land China has grabbed in South America, but that would not be accurate. Its land purchases have been primarily in other Asian nations such as Cambodia and Laos, and an astonishing number of acres in fifteen different African nations. It is unlikely to be accidental that its purchases are concentrated in countries where the rule of law is feeble, if it exists at all. For example, it has acquired at least 100,000 hectares in the Congo, where civil war has raged for decades. Mozambique has yielded some 200,000 hectares, while Zimbabwe has delivered 100,000. A snapshot of Mozambique's political situation offers the fact that though it has recently discovered natural gas off its coast (which will undoubtedly spur all sorts of shady doings in the energy sector), it has yet to be developed. The country is permanently poised on the brink of civil war and most of the population is illiterate. Zimbabwe is home to the infamous leader Robert Mugabe, who has maintained an iron-fisted rule over the country since 1980. It is not hard to imagine where the money went in that transaction. These types of arrangements are by no means the exclusive territory of the Chinese.

Most of the EU countries have also purchased arable land in South America and in Africa, often in former colonies. As the EU countries continue to support more livestock agriculture, the ability to feed their animal populations has to be acquired through some means beyond actually buying grain on the open market. It should be noted that quite a lot of this land is destined for the dual purpose of animal feed and biofuels.

The USA in tandem with various corporations now has control over roughly nine million hectares in 36 countries. What the Matrix doesn't show are sales in more developed industrialized countries such as the United States. Yes, even the mighty USA is not immune to foreign nations scooping up agricultural assets. Saudi Arabia and other Middle Eastern countries or food companies are buying farmland in Arizona and southern California for growing alfalfa to feed their dairy cattle.[5] Canada has availed itself of the relative ease with which American agricultural assets can be acquired, mostly in the form of timberland. The Netherlands and the UK are also big buyers of U.S. assets. More than 25 million acres of American farm, ranch and timberland are owned by foreign countries.[6] Those assets are often located in areas where water shortages are escalating rapidly, such as Arizona, California and Texas. Though water is well regulated in some areas, in Arizona it's a first come, first served free for all. Whoever drills the deepest the fastest will get those precious reserves of water. And of course, the famous Smithfield sale to WH Group in China included 460 farms, in addition to the processing and production facilities.

Though the USA seems oblivious to the ramifications of selling off agricultural assets, others are not so sanguine. Brazil, Argentina and Uruguay have put some brakes on the boom in agricultural land sales in South America. They have not gone so far as to ban foreign acquisition, but they do limit the number of hectares that can be purchased by any one entity. They also limit acquisitions to 25 per cent of any given county or municipality, presumably to curtail foreign influence on local governance. The Australians are following suit, despite recent sales of large properties. In the summer of 2015, negotiations were underway for the sale of an immense property spanning 101,000 square km, or 1.3 per cent of the Australian land mass, to a Chinese firm. Because some of the property abutted a weapons-testing area, the sale was scuttled by the government for national security reasons. That near-miss prompted a review of sales to foreigners, and the government has now set up a registry of foreign holdings in Australia. While most of the country remains firmly in Australian hands, there are many other Chinese, Americans, Japanese and South Koreans who are circling the waters around Australia, looking to snap up some of that rangeland.

As countries respond to the reality of finite resources and a growing population, the impact of food security and food sovereignty assumes a defining role in governance and finance. Crops that feed large corporate interests such as biofuels and meat are replacing the food crops that we all require to stay alive. This trend is a powder keg waiting to blow up the world. As trade agreements proliferate without addressing the underlying failures of providing food security, particularly in developing nations, it is likely we will see famine, unrest and starvation on a wide scale. All so we can feed the pig, the cow and the chicken.

10
ASIA AND THE INDUSTRIALIZED MODEL OF MEAT PRODUCTION

In 1995 Lester Brown published *Who Will Feed China? Wake Up Call for a Small Planet*. Founder of the Worldwatch Institute and the founder and president of the Earth Policy Institute, Brown is legendary for his accurate predictions and analyses of environmental problems and trends. In *Who Will Feed China?*, he proposed that as the Chinese population continued to grow, the need for more cropland to produce food would become critical. What he did not completely foresee was the rapid acceleration of industrialized meat production in China that requires ever more land to raise food for cattle, pigs and chickens. Since the publication of Brown's book, the Chinese have embarked on a systematic reformation of their agricultural programmes with an aim to become food-secure and self-sufficient. For a time they succeeded in growing enough grain to support their population. Now, with the increasing importance placed on meat in the diet, they can no longer produce enough to feed their domestic pork and poultry operations, and they are forced to import great quantities of soy and corn. In addition, as we have seen in previous chapters, they have turned to acquiring and leasing land in other nations as a way to guarantee their food supply. The purchase of the

Smithfield company provides more security in being able to deliver a steady food supply even as their own capacity tops out, or diminishes due to urbanization and water shortages. The entrance of the Chinese as a major player in the world grain market will undoubtedly have profound implications for price and supply going forward.

The Chinese population stands at 1,380,250,973, or 18.74 per cent of the world population. India's population is 1,321,674,066, a very close second. Together they account for nearly half of the humans on this planet. Right now both countries are on an almost vertical trajectory of economic and social development that should be considered unprecedented.

Despite their vastly different histories, they share a few similarities. The majority of their respective citizenries remain on the land, where agriculture is still the most widespread occupation. How the two nations are choosing to develop their agricultural economies is also significantly similar in one very important respect. Both societies are transitioning from a rice-based diet to one that incorporates infinitely more meat. Thus there are massive transformations afoot in how food is raised, and who is doing the raising.

Up until very recently, meat production in most Asian and South Asian regions has been almost exclusively the purview of smallholder farmers who use livestock not just for food but as a means to acquire further wealth, either as collateral for small loans, or to barter for labour, or simply as a hedge against a failed crop or harvest. Virtually every agrarian family owns or owned a flock of chickens, a pig or two, and a buffalo or cow for labour, meat and milk. The chickens foraged around the home, the pigs were fed household slops, and cows or buffalo grazed in commonly used local lands. This model has been in place for centuries throughout the area.

Over the course of the last few decades, both nations have developed a robust middle-class sector, with dietary aspirations that mimic the West. Thanks to the encroachment of Western fast-food restaurants with menus almost exclusively based on animal proteins, the taste for meat has accelerated. When Yum! Brands, owner of Taco Bell, Pizza Hut and Kentucky Fried Chicken (KFC), opened in China in 1987, it took almost no time for the company to install over 6,000 KFC outlets in 1,100 cities. The appetite for fried chicken appeared inexhaustible. Yum! went on to establish a presence in India as well, though they were not as spectacularly successful there. McDonald's followed suit, and East and Southeast Asia became immensely lucrative new markets for those chains. In more recent years, the demographic has changed and tastes are evolving. New 'quick service restaurants' more reflective of the indigenous cultures are developing organically to feed a younger and more sophisticated population. Though the taste for those Western chains may have declined somewhat, it has left behind an appetite for meat that has galvanized the industry.

China's agricultural economy shifted from communes in 1978 to individual farmers who were permitted to sell directly into the market. This allowed them to profit personally from their work. Soon thereafter, foreign investment was allowed, and, once there was more money to throw around, agriculture in general, and poultry and pork in particular, took off. From 1997 to 2009 the production of chicken swelled from about 10 million tonnes to something approaching 18 million tonnes, nearly doubling in size and at the same time moving from backyard poultry growers to large intensive farming similar to that in other industrialized nations such as the USA and Brazil.[1]

In 2001 China sought out the guidance of the American poultry giant Tyson to help develop the practices that offer standardized, cleaner, safer and more predictable chickens. Tyson brought in a fully vertically integrated system with its own genetics, the standard white-feathered bird. They built a feed mill, grow-out houses, processing plants and production facilities to cut up, bread, cook or otherwise transform poultry into ready-to-eat meals destined for grocery stores and fast food. Bringing in Western know-how opened the floodgates of production, and the small-scale farmers have all but disappeared unless they are breeding niche or organic birds, a very small sector of the industry.

While the intense integration of the American poultry industry has not yet been achieved, the government and the industry are pushing farmers into co-op groups or into contracts that mimic American practices in most ways. Many farmers in China now house tens of thousands of birds. China is ranked second in broiler production worldwide. As food safety scandals have proliferated, the Chinese government has encouraged not only Tyson but BRF (Brasil Foods) and Marfrig to set up plants and to contract with local farmers. To date, most Chinese still prefer to purchase their meat in 'wet markets' where they can pick out their own bird and see it slaughtered on the spot.[2] However, 'wet markets' are being discouraged as vectors for food-borne illness. Using that safety rationale, industrial companies and the government are encouraging the purchase of packaged or frozen brands. With a population that has never before subscribed to the notion of processed foods, this has been a tough sell for corporations. The many recent and not so recent food safety scandals in China have boosted their cause.

The adoption of the Western model of animal production has major implications for Asia. With the former smallholder being encouraged to either 'get big or get out', as former U.S. agriculture secretary Earl Butz would have suggested, that means fewer farmers are competing. The downward pressure on prices for chicken conferred by large-scale intensive operations ushers small producers out of the industry. This same model applies to pork as well, another sector that is being recast in the American mould. Adopting American/ Western models comes with all the same problems that are endemic to intensive livestock production in any country. Fouling waterways, polluting soil and releasing methane and other greenhouse gases are all part of the cost of doing business à la Tyson. As noted in an earlier chapter, the rapid growth of the livestock industry has rendered over half of China's water unpotable, and a good bit of their arable land contaminated.

What drives the aggregation of small businesses into larger ones is in part the Chinese government's designation of companies that qualify as 'dragon heads'. These businesses are meant to harness the many smaller farms into larger entities producing products that the 'dragon head' will then market and distribute to other areas of

China, or other countries. A company will acquire dragon head status when it meets certain criteria for success set by the government. It's a complex system meant to support a farming model that attempts to mimic a Smithfield or Tyson. Scores of smaller farms have gone under as a result, and rural poverty remains extreme in many parts of China. At this point nearly 70 per cent of meat production appears to be in the hands of dragon head businesses. These companies have close ties with local and regional governments and supply about two-thirds of urban food needs.[3] Dragon head companies also buy and sell other companies, including those from the West, such as feed mills and grain dealers, as part of the overall scheme to vertically integrate food production on a massive scale.

The dragon head system has been quite successful in the sense that access to food in urban areas has increased exponentially since the inception of the policy in the mid-1990s. That is not the whole picture, however. The dragon head companies control the prices of feed, medications and price per pound, as is typical of Western contract farming models. What is different is that they sell the chicks (rather than maintaining ownership of the bird), feed and medicine to farmers, and then buy back the chickens when they are mature. Similar to the contract farmer in the West, the prices are variable, and a farmer won't know how much he will get per bird until the dragon head sets the price. Once the dragon head buys the bird, they sell it into grocery chains and quick service restaurants (QSRs).

With the same pressures to produce as are found in other contract formats, chicken farmers are equally anxious to turn a profit. In 2012 this anxiety brought about an overuse of antibiotics and growth hormones (banned in poultry in the USA) in what were dubbed Instant Chickens by the media. Birds were growing to 5 lb (2.3 kg) in forty days, a result that even Tyson cannot produce. KFC discovered it was selling chicken with dangerous drug residues remaining in the carcasses, and a major scandal ensued, resulting in profound losses for the chain and the parent company Yum! In the race to grow their birds faster, KFC chicken suppliers were busted for administering up to eighteen different antibiotics along with other chemicals. Recognizing the difficulty of inspecting and testing chickens from so many different small producers, the restaurant dropped at least 1,000 small farms from its supply chain, moving to growers with more transparency who would adopt methods dictated by the restaurant chain. Scandals like this continue to marginalize small farms and reward the larger, more Westernized businesses increasingly favoured by dragon head firms and the government.[4]

Pointing the finger at smaller producers for food safety issues such as drug residues or food-borne illness outbreaks deflects attention away from the by-products of industrial meat production. Farmers wouldn't need to use anything like the current amounts of antibiotics in their animals if they were not trying to keep up with the industrial-scale model. The real culprit in all of this is the Western ideal of intensive livestock production with all its attendant ills, not the smallholder whose traditional methods have served for centuries past. The change in diet is changing the society, the land and the national economy.

With trade barriers dissolving between Asian nations, the Chinese are capitalizing on not just their own increasing taste for meat, but that of their near neighbours. Thailand, Vietnam, Cambodia and Laos are opening more QSRs that will require ever greater numbers of those big white-feathered birds so ideally suited to intensive production. The local indigenous breeds, tastier and far more robust, are still in demand, but they won't work for the packaged, frozen, processed products the Chinese government and the West tout as 'progress'. As an example, a major franchisee is planning to open a hundred new McDonald's outlets in Vietnam in the next few years. McNuggets for all!

The Chinese love pork above all other meats, and it is in China that the Western model of intensive production has soared. By investing heavily in American methods, genetics and protocols including food safety, the Chinese government, through its acquisition of Smithfield, demonstrated that it is committed to eliminating the types of food safety and food fraud scandals that have rocked China in the last few years. The growth of the pork sector has mimicked the consolidation in the USA of pork farming. As recently as two decades ago, 70 per cent of pork in China was grown by small farmers with just a few pigs each, typically around ten. Since then the rise of dragon head enterprises has contributed to forcing the small players out and rewarding those that either work in large co-ops or simply scale up. In 2015, 70 per cent of the pork in China was raised in confinement by large, and larger, producers, a total reverse of centuries of husbandry.[5]

Not surprisingly, the rapid industrialization of pork (and poultry) production did not arise with commensurate know-how or state-of-the-art facilities. The aforementioned 'Instant Chicken' was just one of many meat-related scandals that have plagued the Chinese public in the last decade, and contributed mightily to the adoption of the CAFO model. Small-scale farmers raising backyard pigs have been tarred with the same brush as small poultry producers as vectors for disease and unsanitary practices. What seems to be missing from the analysis is the understanding that the model itself of confining tens or hundreds of thousands of animals in small spaces leads to its own spectrum of animal diseases and associated public health and environmental problems.

Domestic pork production in China dwarfs that of the rest of the world. They are growing and processing half of the world's pork supply. Their production is five times what is produced in the United States, and twice as much as is produced in all of the EU countries combined.[6] In real terms, that means that the Chinese are producing nearly 800 million pigs a year. Thinking back to what a fraction of that number of pigs delivers in waste demonstrates the real breakdown in the concentrated area-feeding operation model. What can they do with all the shit? Well aware of the massive problems this poses and the immense impact on agriculture, the government is working very hard to find ways of dealing with effluent. Some Chinese firms are investing heavily in covered anaerobic digesters and other means of cleaning up the sanitation issues, but there is no silver bullet for dealing with billions of tons of toxic waste, loaded with antibiotics, hormones and heavy metals such as copper, arsenic, zinc and cadmium.

All the government subsidies in the world (and the Chinese heavily subsidize the growth of their meat industry in all sorts of ways) will not solve this problem any time soon. In their battle to convince the population that the government can and will deliver safe, fresh and cost-effective food, the experts, both Western and Eastern entities, have failed to address the fundamental flaws in the CAFO form of production. It will be up to the Chinese people to recognize and begin to correct the agricultural disaster that is big meat.

Infrastructure

Creating a meat supply chain is a complex and costly business and that is the paramount reason why Western meat companies are so enthusiastically welcomed into Asian nations. They offer systems that are economically efficient and, compared with many local suppliers, can be safer. Pork production in the USA is cheaper by about 20 cents a pound than it is in China because of the ample supplies of corn and soy located right next to feedlots. In addition, food safety issues remain a major and ongoing problem in Chinese and Indian meat production because of the lack of a reliable 'cold chain'. Many local markets lack refrigeration. Transporting meat safely from one area to another is also problematic because of a dearth of refrigerated trucks or train cars. With the kind of vast travel distances in both countries, this presents a major obstacle to developing the distribution system prevalent in more developed countries.

Often when a foreign firm is involved in establishing a plant or production facility, the investment will include some infrastructural investments such as improving roads or bringing in refrigerated transportation. This type of investment can certainly be a boon to a developing country, and especially so if one looks at it from a Western perspective. But assuming that having a large grocery store packed with processed and frozen foods is the ideal system is to ignore the many problems that system has brought to Western populations, including the higher incidence of heart disease, diabetes and obesity that characterizes that style of food procurement. The current and most prevalent way of purchasing food in Asian countries is that of the open market with live birds and fish, and the day's slaughter of cattle or hogs, along with grains, legumes and whatever fruits and vegetables are seasonal. Packaged and processed foods are relatively rare in a market such as this, though certainly they exist to some extent. It seems a very unfortunate strategy to dispense with a system that has functioned for millennia in order to establish an industry that is profitable for a few, and undeniably damaging for many.

India

As the second-place leader in world population, India too is anxious to become a major dealer in animal proteins. The eating of meat, eggs and dairy is enthusiastically encouraged by the government in an effort to counter the widespread hunger and malnutrition that continues to plague so much of the population, despite the improving economy of the last three decades. India still sees a significant portion of the population as food-insecure (estimates are difficult to make for various reasons, but USDA figures propose some 255 million people), so the impetus for growing a calorie- and nutritionally rich resource such as beef (and poultry and dairy) is obviously compelling.[7] Developing the meat industry further is a major economic goal as well. Still hampered by a lack of facilities and of a reliable cold chain, growth is somewhat fitful, but foreign and private investment in new modern abattoirs is growing. The expanding market for Indian beef in the Middle East, Vietnam and China, a recently opened market, will certainly spur production sharply. India has invested in halal butchering practices as well, much as Brazil has, and this has really paid off for them in both the domestic and export markets.

India is, in fact, the world's largest exporter of beef, from buffalo. The whopping U.S.$4.8 billion figure is surprising since the domestic consumer is so very different from their counterpart in other meat-producing nations.[8] Though 70 per cent of Indians consume meat, regional tastes and conventions vary greatly. As the most obvious example of this bifurcation of the meat market overall, one need only look at the two major religious groups. Hindus consider the cow to be sacred, while Muslims abhor pork. At the same time there are many other groups that have their own tastes in meat and don't participate in the industry at all, preferring to keep and slaughter their own animals, such as goats, sheep and rabbits.

The battle over beef in India is heating up, under the government of Narendra Modi and his mostly Hindu party. A very outspoken anti-beef activist in the past, Modi has not made any great effort thus far to protect the industry or to discourage violence against those who are in the business. Just in the last year or two there have been a number of violent incidents where Hindus have attacked and even killed people they believe to have slaughtered cows for sale. Most recently, in 2015, a ban on the slaughter of any bovine has been instituted in two large Indian states, a reflection of the local sentiment for their cows. Some more right-wing members of the government and population at large are calling for a national ban on buffalo and cattle slaughter altogether. If that ban were to pass, estimates put the loss to the economy at roughly 2 per cent of gross domestic product (GDP).[9]

There is also a very large dairy herd in India, but most of the spent dairy cows are sent to old age homes established for them by Hindu populations. No doubt there is a thriving 'grey' market, an underground channel for slaughtering, processing and selling some of these cows into other countries such as Bangladesh, where the fervour for the sacred nature of the cow comes nowhere near the fervour for cheap meat. Figures for how much meat is produced through these informal arrangements and how much money is at stake are well-nigh impossible to come by, but when examining figures for export vs agricultural censuses on buffalo and dairy cows there are distinct discrepancies between how many animals exist and how much meat is being exported.

Indians have the world's largest populations of water buffalo and it is this beast that forms the backbone of their cattle industry. While beef from water buffalo is not the same quality as American, Brazilian or Australian beef, it is much in demand from Vietnam and Middle Eastern countries where growing cattle is not an option. Many countries are keen on India's buffalo beef because it has been grown on grass and, as a relatively unorganized business, there are fewer if any inputs such as bovine growth hormones, antibiotics, beta agonists and other measures common to Western production. Thus even though some Indians may be loath to eat beef for religious reasons, the numbers are growing for domestic consumption in addition to the export market.

Poultry, on the other hand, is religiously neutral. As a result, it has become a major industry in India, moving from backyard flocks to indoor production in the style of the West. India is now the fourth-largest producer of broiler chickens in the world. With that comes the inevitable loss of genetic variety in favour of the Western breeds that grow fast and can withstand the exigencies of confined production. The transition from backyard to factory production in India comes with the same set of problems as anywhere else.

The whole system of contract farming is gaining traction in India, where farmers who may have once had a few hundred birds are now growing out tens of thousands. Ninety-three per cent of the birds are destined for live markets, which puts some brakes on how far they can be transported safely. Indeed the distribution of meat in general is heavily weighted toward urban centres, where residents generally eat roughly twice as much meat as those in rural areas. Mimicking the West, the majority of the poultry industry is controlled by just five firms who employ roughly 60,000 farmers in raising their birds.[10] Whether employment figures will continue to rise is questionable. If one uses the West as a yardstick, chances are the farms will get bigger and more automated, needing fewer people to actually work on the farms. What will continue to expand will be the ancillary industries of pharmaceuticals, feed mills and veterinarian services. Assuming Indians eventually accept packaged meats, there will be a commensurate growth in processing jobs.

What has greatly aided the rise in industrialized poultry production besides the increased demand is that India has traditionally grown corn. Once consumed directly by people, now it is mostly consumed by chickens. The increase in planting corn has allowed the industry to expand quickly and economically since it is now less reliant on imports and the vagaries of supply and demand on the world market. As the poultry sector grows, it is expected that the production of corn, and to some extent soy, will increase as well. The expanding demand for corn and soy is boosting another sector of the agricultural economy, leading to more demand for animal proteins as former subsistence farmers begin to earn more from cultivating competitively priced crops that feed the meat industry.

Even with increased planting, India is lagging in corn production from the point of view of capitalizing on improved yields from hybridized or genetically modified organism (GMO) products purchased from the West. The agricultural industry is investing in research and development to remedy the knowledge gap regarding seeds and technology so they can continue to keep pace with the development of not just the broiler industry but the enormous number of laying hens, now ranking third in production behind the USA and China. The meat and feed giant Cargill has a division in India and is bringing in new seed technology as well. The country has only recently begun trading corn futures on its commodities market.[11] In total, 51 per cent of the corn crop in India is now going into poultry feed, with another 17 per cent allocated for cattle and 23 per cent consumed directly by people. Commodity trading in futures on grains and cereals has caused major food shortages and political upheavals in the past. How this will play out in an Indian context remains to be seen. The bottom line is that as their chicken business grows, whether in laying hens or in broilers, the country will need to grow more and more corn. Will that all-important corn crop supplant food crops for the Indian population? Will Indian farmers fall prey to the same problems intensive monocropping has caused in the USA for example, where the need for intensive fertilizer and pest control contributes to loss of fertility, pollution of waterways and a new crop of superweeds? It certainly seems possible.

What is most evident is that two major population centres are ratcheting up a Western system of food procurement that is rapidly demonstrating itself to be more of a disaster and less of a miracle than the world ever imagined. Turning arable land that grows crops for people into land growing crops for animals often destined for export seems a poor bargain for a developing country, however profitable the equation may seem in the short term. Displacement of traditional customs and mores may have consequences these two ancient cultures have not foreseen in their quest to 'modernize'. Raising populations up from poverty and want is surely a noble ambition. It is to be hoped that those same populations take the time to observe and learn from the examples of their Western neighbours what methods can truly improve quality of life and livelihood, and discard the notions that have clearly failed.

CONCLUSION

Is it any wonder that people are questioning the major role of meat in the diet when the problems endemic to industrialized meat production are so daunting? The industry presents itself as the salvation for a hungry world, but, as we have seen, in its present form it clearly creates more problems than it solves.

On the plus side, industrialized meat production makes it possible for more people than ever before to enjoy the gastronomic pleasures and nutritional advantages of incorporating meat into their lifestyle. The industry supports a vast chain of employment, from the farmers and ranchers who grow the animals and the grain, to those who work in pharmaceuticals, veterinary sciences and genetics, to the labourers who toil in processing and production, and everyone in between. The export trade for major meat-producing nations is a major source of revenue, adding to overall GDP. On the surface there is a lot to love about the meat business.

Unfortunately the downsides to the industry are many and frustrating. This is a giant agro-industrial complex that exercises its power to influence trade agreements and treaties, subvert legislation and hold politicians hostage to its agenda. Meat companies have demonstrated a ruthless disregard for the environment, for animal welfare and for workers, despite their vigorous protestations to the contrary. The global reach of the biggest players such as JBS or Tyson has profound impacts on developing nations, as they extend their model into new territory. Selling the idea of meat as a route to prosperity in poor nations, their presence disrupts centuries-old agricultural practices, forcing changes in crop production and land use in order to feed the animals. By cutting deals with corrupt or ignorant government officials, they push small farmers off their land through land grabs, or out of business by undercutting local prices, a phenomenon made possible only by the vertical integration and economies of scale central to industrialized production.

On another level, many scientists and university departments depend on industry largesse for grants to continue their research in animal, plant and pharmaceutical sciences. Research findings liked by the industry are touted heavily as proof of its success. Anything less can be publicly discredited or simply suppressed. Thus not only have the companies penetrated the heart of rural communities, but they hold sway in agricultural academia as well.

The monopolistic nature of the industry is deeply problematic. With just a handful of companies essentially controlling the global production of meat, food supplies are increasingly the purview of the well to do, while the poor are left with fewer options and less land. The focus on singular breedstocks is also a dangerous path to pursue. For example, the financial and practical impact of recent outbreaks of bird flu in the USA and China sent the price of eggs sky high. That alone should be enough to convince the industry that having more than one type of bird is simply common sense as a hedge against disease. Food shortages and food insecurity are political disasters as well as humanitarian crises.

Consumer demands have forced the industry to protect animals more effectively from hardship or abuse, but it took the emergence of YouTube and the ubiquitous presence of smartphones with cameras to make that happen. Phasing out gestation crates for pigs and battery cages for laying hens is a major step forward in improving conditions for industrially produced livestock. Many companies now have third-party-audited video cameras in their animal-handling facilities to monitor welfare. Companies such as Perdue and Tyson are phasing antibiotics out of their chickens. Cargill has abandoned the use of beta agonists. These changes represent encouraging acknowledgement and acceptance of consumer demands. Credit should also be given to McDonald's for hiring Dr Temple Grandin to design better animal-handling and -slaughtering techniques for cattle, a move brought about as much by economic considerations as by welfare concerns. With ever more pressure from institutional buyers such as McDonald's, Chipotle and Whole Foods in response to consumer demands, the industry is being forced to upgrade its role in 'humane' treatment.

More changes are on the way, whether the industry wants them or not. With all of the meat industry consolidation that has taken place, financial companies are heavily involved in mergers, acquisitions, land deals and expansions. Agricultural investments have become more common in the wake of the financial meltdown and the recession in 2007–8. As illustrated by the TIAA-Cref scandal in Brazil described in Chapter Nine, as well as the influence of Goldman Sachs and others in the acquisition of Smithfield by the Chinese, banks and investment companies are taking positions that come with a whole new set of risks not typically found in more conventional investments. Considerations such as political changes in subsidy structures, water shortages, environmental problems or disease epidemics should all be factors in an investor's mind when considering committing capital to the meat industry. A report from the Farm Animal Investment Risk and Return (FAIRR), an investment initiative from the Jeremy Coller Foundation, identified 28 separate categories of what they describe as 'environmental, social, and governance issues', or ESGs.[1] The report suggests that failing to take into account the ESGs of the meat industry would amount to fiduciary irresponsibility. As investors become more aware of the threats to profit represented by the ESGs, pressure will mount on the industry to make greater improvements. Even now shareholders are making demands for environmental stewardship that extends well beyond just reducing water use or retooling packaging.

For decades, the meat business was able to keep a very low profile as it developed its current model of contracts, consolidation and confinement. That opacity has diminished over the last decade as consumers have pressed for more information about how their food is produced. The overuse of antibiotics, animal welfare issues and the environmental impacts of the CAFO model have drawn enormous and unwanted public scrutiny. The FAIRR report shows the weaknesses in the current model, from an economic and investment standpoint, and the industry overall must address these in a more urgent fashion than it has thus far, or it will lose credibility as an investment opportunity.

In 2015 the non-profit investment analyst group Ceres published a report called *Feeding Ourselves Thirsty* in which they evaluated the preparedness for water shortages of a variety of food companies.[2] The results showed a truly dismal lack of awareness for dealing with an inevitable outcome of climate change that will have a major impact on food production in every sector. As a result of the report, many of the profiled companies have taken on advisors or created new 'sustainability' roles in their companies. Prodding by Ceres, the Jeremy Coller Foundation and a host of other organizations is helping to move companies along in thinking strategically about how they use water, manage waste and improve their overall impact on the environment. However, the drive to seek profit seems to have blinded their management to the realities of our changing world.

What is especially discouraging about the meat industry is that many of its cohort seem unconvinced by climate science and unwilling to invest their considerable profits in forward-thinking practices. Even the move to better animal welfare protocols has been glacially slow, pursued reluctantly and only in response to consumer outrage. Instead, the focus is on developing in other countries, exporting a model that has been demonstrated to be at best deeply flawed and at worst criminal. It's a peculiar phenomenon that an industry that seeks to expand globally remains remarkably tone deaf and even defiantly resistant to any change, much less improvement.

The most glaring example of the boneheaded obstinacy of the meat industry is the persistent use of sub-therapeutic antibiotics for growth promotion. This practice, discredited though it has been, makes it clear that the industry puts profit before people by playing fast and loose with the medical arsenal on which the world relies. Countless studies from hundreds of sources have confirmed the dangers of this practice, correctly identifying the profligate use of antibiotics in livestock as a public health emergency. Strains of common food-borne illness-causing bacteria such as *Salmonella* or *E. coli* have evolved into new forms that only exist in the context of industrially produced meat, a direct result of overuse of antibiotics. Yet the practice remains common, even if it is called 'disease prevention' instead of 'growth promotion'. Clearly there is something very wrong with a system in which animals will perish from disease if their drugs are taken away. Only a few countries in the world have committed to stop using antibiotics for anything but treating disease. Despite the European success in weaning their animals from prophylactic antibiotic use, many companies in the USA, Brazil, China, India and elsewhere continue to abuse these precious drugs to compensate for failures in hygiene and husbandry.

Waste management is another area in which the industry has demonstrated complete disregard for the communities in which it is situated. Frequently fined for groundwater pollution by failed containment systems or agricultural run-off, the top executives behave quasi-feudally as if they have a right to jeopardize property values and water supplies by failing to manage their effluent. Though they have been outrageously successful in passing the clean-up costs onto the taxpayer, that strategy cannot prevail indefinitely. Eventually, either legislation will force the industry to pay full freight for its air, water and soil pollution or investors will desert it, depriving it of capital. As noted in Chapter Four, Cargill has built processing plants that include covered anaerobic digesters. The digesters eat up all the bacteria while harnessing the methane for energy use in the plant. But only a very wealthy company can invest the millions required for that kind of technology. For the contract farmers who raise the animals, without financial assistance there is simply no remedy beyond aggregating the manure into ponds and spraying it on fields. The method does not represent a viable solution to waste management, and it is where taxpayers bear the burden when something goes wrong. Companies must step up and provide the technology to farmers so they are not held responsible for a problem that by rights should be owned by the parent company.

The one irrefutable reason that CAFOs cannot succeed in the long term is this: there simply is not enough arable land to grow the feed crops required. As the population continues to increase, less land will be available for farming overall. The world cannot subsist on meat alone. Every last centimetre of arable land would have to be planted to feed crops destined to sustain the livestock population envisioned by the meat industry. Livestock, pasture and the crops needed to feed animals already account for 80 per cent of the world's arable land.[3]

Climate change will bring water shortages that will render corn and soy production impractical. Though seed companies such as Monsanto and Dupont are developing new drought-resistant varieties of many crops, it seems folly to depend on that as a strategy for feeding the world.

Ultimately it is neither reasonable nor realistic to assume that an industry as large and complex as this one can or even should be dismantled. Nor is it realistic to suppose that returning to small-scale farming will be adequate to meet the needs of the nine billion people who will be sharing Planet Earth in 2050. Developing nations have the same right to a ready source of affordable animal protein as the rest of us.

Instead, governments, and agricultural interests including the meat industry, can and indeed must begin to invest serious money into research that promotes a more agro-ecological model. Incorporating the efficiencies and technological advances that have brought us this far into a system that promotes better use of natural resources is the only solution to providing the world with the food necessary to sustain life. I do not pretend to know what that system would look like, but I do know that food production as it is practised now, particularly in the livestock sector, is doomed. Our future depends on the willingness of the agro-industrial complex to address the failures of the current model and move into new practices that will ensure the survival of our species and our planet.

REFERENCES

INTRODUCTION

1 'Meat and Animal Feed', www.globalagriculture.org.
2 Carol Helstocky, *The SAGE Encyclopedia of Food Issues* (London, 2015), pp. 38–41.
3 Michael Bloch, 'Fast Facts – Meat Consumption Statistics', www.greenlivingtips.com, May 2012.
4 Georgi Gyton, 'JBS Posts Record Revenue for 2014', *Global Meat News*, www.globalmeatnews.com, 2 April 2015.
5 Jacob Bunge, 'Tyson Foods Beats Profit Expectations', *Wall Street Journal*, www.wsj.com, 5 February 2016.

1 THE EVOLUTION OF INDUSTRIALIZED MEAT PRODUCTION

1 Stephanie Paige Ogburn, 'Cattlemen Struggle against Meatpackers and Economic Squeezes', *High Country News*, March 2011.
2 European Commission, Agriculture and Rural Development, 'Poultry', www.ec.europa.eu, 2014.
3 CDC, 'Antibiotic Use in Food-producing Animals', www.cdc.gov/narms/animals, accessed 9 September 2016.
4 Fiona Fleck, 'What to Do about Resistant Bacteria in the Food Chain', *Bulletin of the World Health Organization*, XCIII (2015), pp. 217–18.
5 Dr Margaret Chan, 'Remarks at the G7 Health Ministers Meeting. Session on Antimicrobial Resistance: Realizing the "One Health" Approach', www.who.int, 8 October 2015.
6 Dr Urvashi Rangan, direct quote from an interview on 'What Doesn't Kill You: Food Industry Insights' on Heritage Radio Network.org, episode 67, 3 May 2013.

7 'Empire of the Pig: China's Insatiable Appetite for Pork', *The Economist*, www.economist.com, 20 December 2014.
8 Mark Godfrey, 'Northern China to See Significant Investment in Poultry Sector', *Global Meat News*, www.globalmeatnews.com, June 2015.
9 Adam Minter, 'China Needs to Prevent Antibiotic Apocalypse', www.bloombergview.com, 23 November 2015.
10 National Research Council, Committee on Drug Use in Food Animals, Panel on Animal Health, Food Safety, and Public Health, *The Use of Drugs in Food Animals: Benefits and Risks* (Washington, DC, 1999), p. 31.
11 Simon A. Levin, 'Global Trends in Antimicrobial Use in Food Animals', *Proceedings of the National Academy of Sciences*, www.princeton.edu, February 2015.
12 John Ikerd, 'The Economics of CAFOS and Sustainable Alternatives,' web.missouri.edu, October 2009.

2 THE BUSINESS OF GENETICS

1 Susanne Gura, *Livestock Genetics Companies. Concentration and Proprietary Strategies of an Emerging Power in the Global Food Economy* (Ober-Ramstadt, 2007).
2 Institute for Agriculture and Trade Policy, 'Contracted Lives: The Experience of Farmers in the Meat Chain in Brazil, India and the U.S.', IATP Webinar, www.iatp.org, 2015.
3 Michael Moss, 'U.S. Research Lab Lets Animals Suffer in Quest for Profit', *New York Times*, www.nytimes.com, 20 January 2015.
4 Sophia Chen, 'Genetically Modified Animals Will Be on Your Plate in No Time', *Wired*, www.wired.com, 6 July 2015.
5 Chuck Abbot, 'FDA Approves GE Chicken to Produce Human Drug' 12 October 2015, *Ag Insider*, www.fern.org, 10 December 2015.
6 Arielle Duhaim-Ross, 'FDA Approves Genetically Modified Chicken But Not as Food', *The Verge*, www.theverge.com, 9 December 2015.
7 Oscar Rousseau, 'China Plans a Cloning Factory', *Global Meat News*, www.globalmeatnews.com, 26 November 2015.
8 Paulo Cesar Maiorka, Phelipe Oliveira Favaron, Andrea Maria Mess, Caio Rodrigues dos Santos, Miryan Lanca Alberto,

Flavio Vieira Meirelles and Maria Angelica Miglino, 'Vascular Alterations Underlie Developmental Problems Manifested in Cloned Cattle before or after Birth', National Center for Biotechnology Information, www.ncbi.nlm.nih.gov, 13 January 2015.

3 LIVESTOCK AND DISEASE

1 Belinda Cleeland, 'The Bovine Spongiform Encephalopathy (BSE) Epidemic in the United Kingdom', International Risk Governance Council, www.irgc.org, April 2012, p. 1.
2 'BSE and Beef, New Controls Explained', Food Standards Agency, www.food.gov.uk 2015, p. 3.
3 C. R. Hamilton, 'Real and Perceived Issues Involving Animal Protein', Food and Agriculture Organization of the United Nations, www.fao.org, 2015.
4 'The 2009 H1N1 Pandemic: Summary Highlights, April 2009–April 2010', Centers for Disease Control and Prevention, www.cdc.gov, 16 June 2010.
5 'First Global Estimates of 2009 H1N1 Pandemic Mortality Released by CDC-led Collaboration', Centers for Disease Control and Prevention, www.cdc.gov, 25 June 2012.
6 Stephanie Nebehay, 'China's Bird Flu Outbreak Cost $6.5 Billion', *Reuters*, 21 May 2013, www.reuters.com.
7 'WHO Estimates of the Global Burden of Foodborne Diseases', World Health Organisation, www.who.int, 2015, pp. 1–3.
8 Ibid.
9 S. E. Majowicz, E. Scallan, A. Jones-Bitton, J. M. Sargeant, J. Stapleton, F. J. Angulo, D. H. Yeun and M. D. Kirk, 'Global Incidence of Human Shiga Toxin-producing Escherichia Coli Infections and Deaths: A Systematic Review and Knowledge Synthesis', National Center for Biotechnology Information, www.ncbi.nlm.nih.gov, 21 April 2014.
10 James Andrews, 'Jack in the Box and the Decline of E.coli', *Food Safety News*, www.foodsafetynews.com, 11 February 2013.
11 Ibid.
12 Dan Flynn, 'USDA: U.S. Foodborne Illnesses Cost More Than $15.6 Billion Annually', *Food Safety News*, www.foodsafetynews.com, 9 October 2014.

13 'EFSA: Campylobacter and Listeria Cases Rise Again in the European Union', *Food Safety News*, www.foodsafetynews.com, 17 December 2015.
14 Caroline Smith DeWaal and Nadine Robert, 'Global and Local: Food Safety Around the World', Center for Science in the Public Interest, www.cspinet.org, June 2005, p. 36.
15 Yanzhong Huang, 'China's Worsening Food Safety Crisis', *The Atlantic*, www.theatlantic.com, 28 August 2012.
16 'Salmonella, Non-Typhoidal', WHO Media Centre, www.who.int, Fact Sheet #139, August 2013.
17 'Dangerous Contaminated Chicken', *Consumer Reports*, www.consumerreports.org, February 2014.
18 Henrik Wegener, 'Antibiotic Resistance – Linking Human and Animal Health', National Center for Biotechnology Information, bookshelf #NBK114485, www.ncbi.nlm.nih.gov, 2012.
19 'What Is Campylobacteriosis?', Centers for Disease Control and Prevention, www.cdc.gov, June 2014.
20 'What Is Campylobacter?', European Food Safety Authority, www.efsa.europa.eu, January 2015.
21 'EFSA: Campylobacter and Listeria Cases Rise Again in the EU', *Food Safety News*, www.foodsafetynews.com, 17 December 2015.
22 James Andrews, 'WHO Study Measures Global Burden of Listeria', *Food Safety News*, www.foodsafetynews.com, 3 October 2014.
23 Maryn McKenna, 'How Your Chicken Dinner Is Creating a Drug Resistant Superbug', *The Atlantic*, www.theatlantic.com, June 2012.
24 Amee R. Manges and James Johnson, 'Food-borne Origins of *Escherichia coli* Causing Extraintestinal Infections', *Oxford Journal of Clinical Infectious Diseases*, LV/5 (August 2012), pp. 712–19, www.oxfordjournals.org.

4 ENVIRONMENTAL COSTS

1 Raychel Santo, 'New FAO Report on Livestock and Climate Change', Johns Hopkins Center for A Livable Future blog, www.livablefutureblog.com, 15 October 2013.
2 James Barker, 'Manure, Myths and Facts: Frequently Asked Questions about Livestock Production', North Carolina State University, www.bae.ncsu.edu, 2015.

3 Douglas Hamilton, William G. Luce and Aimee D. Heald, 'Production and Characteristics of Swine Manure', Oklahoma Cooperative Extension Service, Oklahoma State University, accessed 2015.
4 Robert Chambers, 'Things You Need to Know about Manure Gas', www.thepigsite.com, 28 August 2011.
5 'Precautionary Moratorium on New Concentrated Animal Feed Operations', American Public Health Association, www.apha.org, 24 July 2014.
6 Andrew D. McEachran et al., 'Antibiotics, Bacteria, and Antibiotic Resistance Genes: Aerial Transport from Cattle Feed Yards via Particulate Matter', *Environmental Health Perspectives*, CXXIII/4 (April 2015), http://ehp.niehs.nih.gov.
7 Mary Lee Hultin, Shannon Briggs, Margaret Sadoff, Linda D. Dykema and Brian Hughes, 'Concentrated Animal Feedlot Operations (CAFOs) Chemicals Associated with Air Emissions', Michigan Department of Environmental Quality, www.michigan.gov, 10 May 2006.
8 McEachran et al., 'Antibiotics, Bacteria, and Antibiotic Resistance Genes'.
9 'Arsenic', World Health Organization, www.who.int, December 2012.
10 Aude Teillant, 'Costs and Benefits of Antimicrobial Use in Livestock', *Global Health Dynamics*, www.globalhealthdynamics.co.uk.
11 McEachran et al., 'Antibiotics, Bacteria, and Antibiotic Resistance Genes'.
12 Jennifer Duggan, 'China's Polluters to Face Large Fines under Law Change', *The Guardian*, www.theguardian.com, 25 April 2014.
13 'Livestock's Role in Deforestation', Food and Agriculture Organization of the United Nations, www.fao.org, September 2015.
14 Vincent Ter Beek, 'Swill Feed Could Make Pigs More Sustainable', *Pig Progress*, www.pigprogress.net, 21 December 2015.

5 ANIMAL WELFARE

1 'Recognizing Animal Protection', World Animal Protection, api.worldanimalprotection.org, 2 November 2014.

2 'Welfare Implications of Gestation Sow Housing', American Veterinary Medical Association, www.avma.org, 19 November 2015.
3 Sara Shields and Michael Greger, 'Animal Welfare and Food Safety Aspects of Confining Broiler Chickens to Cages', Humane Society of the United States, www.humanesociety.org, 13 May 2013.
4 'Ractopamine', Food and Water Watch, www.foodandwater-watch.org, April 2013.
5 Deena Shanker, 'Big Beef Keeps Getting Bigger, Thanks to Growth Drugs with Unclear Safety Records', *Fortune*, www.fortune.com, 13 February 2015.
6 The Humane Society of the United States, 'Welfare Issues with the Use of Hormones and Antibiotics in Animal Agriculture', www.humanesociety.org, November 2016.
7 V. Cussen and L. Garces, *Long Distance Transport and Welfare of Farm Animals* (Wallingford, 2008), pp. 345–8.
8 James Menzies, 'USDA Clarifies 28 Hour Law for Livestock Transporters', *Truck News*, www.trucknews.com, 1 November 2006.
9 Agriculture Victoria, 'Land Transport of Livestock Standards and Guidelines', agriculture.vic.gov.au, 2010.
10 M. J. Ritter et al., 'Review: Transport Losses in Market Weight Pigs: I. A Review of Definitions, Incidence, and Economic Impact', *Professional Animal Scientist*, XXV/4 (August 2009), pp. 404–14.
11 Cussen and Garces, *Long Distance Transport and Welfare of Farm Animals*, pp. 345–8.
12 Temple Grandin, 'What Doesn't Kill You: Food Industry Insights', http://heritageradionetwork.org, episode 91.
13 'Recognizing Animal Protection', World Animal Protection, api.worldanimalprotection.org, 2 November 2014.

6 WAGES, WORKERS AND SAFETY ISSUES

1 International Labour Organization, 'International Labour Standards by Subject', www.ilo.org, 2014.
2 Dr Patrick O'Leary, 'Neoliberal Employer Industrial Relations Strategies in the U.S. and Australian Meat Industries', Business School at the University of Ballarat, Australia, www.vu.edu.au, 2012.

3 'Meat and Migrants', *Rural Migration News*, XX/1 (January 2014), migration.ucdavis.edu.
4 Bettina Wagner and Anke Hassel, 'Labor Migration and the German Meat Processing Industry: Fundamental Freedoms and the Influx of Cheap Labor', *South Atlantic Quarterly*, CXIV/1 (January 2015), p. 6.
5 'Germany's Meat Industry Stirs Debate on Low Pay', *Financial Times*, www.ft.com, 2015.
6 Jeroen Beinaert, 'Brazilian Meatpackers Celebrate Landmark Victory on Safety Standards', *Equal Times*, www.equaltimes.org, 7 May 2013; Jeb Blount, 'BRF Workers in Brazil's Mato Grosso Threaten Strike Over Pay', *Reuters*, www.reuters.com, 14 December 2015.
7 Occupational Safety and Health Administration, 'Personal Protective Equipment', United States Department of Labor, www.osha.com, 2015.
8 Oxfam America, 'Lives on the Line, The Human Cost of Cheap Chicken', www.oxfamamerica.org, October 2015.

7 CONCENTRATION AND CONSOLIDATION IN THE INDUSTRY

1 Shefali Sharma et al., 'Industrialized Meat', Institute for Agriculture and Trade Policy, IATP webinar series, www.iatp.org, 2015.
2 Dan Cunningham, 'Contract Broiler Production: Questions and Answers', www.thepoultrysite.com, 30 April 2004.
3 National Chicken Council, 'March Madness – Why Contract Growing in the Chicken Industry Is Not a Tournament', www.nationalchickencouncil.org, 15 March 2012.
4 United States Department of Agriculture, 'Census of Hog and Pig Farming', www.agcensus.usda.gov, June 2014.
5 Regina Weiss, 'Ninety Years On – Will the Feds Finally Break Up the Meat Monopoly?', *Huffington Post*, www.huffingtonpost.com, 30 August 2010.
6 Rupert Steiner, 'No Hen Party for Suffering UK Poultry Firms as Producers Struggle to Make Ends Meet', www.thisismoney.co.uk, 4 March 2013.
7 *The Economist*, 'A Champion for Choice', www.economist.com, 25 August 2012.

8 Arlie Felton-Taylor, 'Senate Committee Examines Effects of the Consolidation of Meat Processing, www.abc.net.au, 4 August 2015.
9 Cattle Council of Australia, 'Senate Inquiry: Effect of Market Consolidation on the Red Meat Processing Sector', www.cattlecouncil.com.au, July 2015.

8 FOOD FRAUD

1 PwC and SSAFE, 'Food Fraud Vulnerability Assessment', p. 3, www.pwc.nl, 2015.
2 Committee on the Environment, Public Health, and Food Safety, 'On the Food Crisis, Fraud in the Food Chain, and the Control thereof' (2013/2091(INI)), www.europarl.europa.eu, 4 December 2013.
3 Mary Creach, 'Horsemeat Scandal Highlights Gaps in Regulation of Our Food Industry', *The Guardian*, www.theguardian.com, 18 January 2013; Felicity Lawrence, 'Horsemeat Burger Scandal: History Repeating Itself', *The Guardian*, www.theguardian.com, 16 January 2013.
4 David I. Ellis, Howbeer Muhamadali, Simon A. Haughey, Christopher T. Elliott and Royston Goodacre, 'Point-and-Shoot: Rapid Quantitative Detection Methods for On-site Food Fraud Analysis – Moving Out of the Laboratory and into the Food Supply Chain', Royal Society of Chemistry, www.rsc.org, September 2015.
5 'European Union Expands COOL Requirements Beyond Beef', *Food Safety News*, www.foodsafetynews.com, 9 April 2015.
6 Henriette Jacobsen, 'BEUC: Food Labelling Should Include Country of Origin for Meat', European Food Safety Commission, www.euractiv.com, 3 September 2014.
7 European Food Safety Commission, 'Close Up on the Meat We Eat: Consumers Want Honest Labels', www.beuc.eu, 4 November 2015.
8 Sara Lewis, 'BEUC Says Stop Consumers Being Duped on Meat Content', www.eurofoodlaw.com, 4 November 2015.
9 Economic Research Council, 'Annual and Cumulative Year-to-Date U.S. Livestock and Meat Trade by Country', Livestock & Meat International Trade Data, www.ers.usda.com, 7 March 2016.

10 Christina Rice, 'What's In Your Food: A Look at Food Fraud', *Food Safety News*, www.foodsafetynews.com, 14 April 2015.
11 Dan Flynn, 'Is U.S. Beef Safe from Europe's Expanding Horsemeat Crisis?', *Food Safety News*, www.foodsafetynews.com, 11 February 2013.
12 Rhodi Lee, 'DNA Testing Shows Some Ground Meat Sold in U.S. Contains Horsemeat', *TechTimes*, www.techtimes.com, 28 August 2015.
13 U.S. Pharmacopeial Convention, www.usp.org, 2015.

9 TRADE DEALS AND LAND GRABS

1 Oxfam, 'Still Banking on Land Grabs: Australia's Four Big Banks and Land Grabs', www.farmlandgrab.org, 15 February 2016.
2 Oxfam, 'Banking on Shaky Ground: Australia's Four Big Banks and Land Grabs', www.oxfam.org, 2014.
3 Simon Romero, 'TIAA-CREF, Investment Giant, Accused of Land Grabs in Brazil', *New York Times*, www.nytimes.com, 17 November 2015.
4 Lorenzo Cotula, 'How Investment Treaties Protect Land Grab Deals', Oxfam, www.farmlandgrab.org, 17 February 2016.
5 Mike Krieger, 'Saudi Arabia is Buying up American Farmland to Export Agricultural Products Back Home', www.zerohedge.com, 17 January 2016.
6 'Foreign Holdings of U.S. Agricultural Land', www.fsa.usda.gov, 2011.

10 ASIA AND THE INDUSTRIALIZED MODEL OF MEAT PRODUCTION

1 Xie Chaioping and Mary A. Marchant, 'Supplying China's Growing Appetite for Poultry', *International Food and Agribusiness Review*, XVIII (2015), Special Issue A, p. 11.
2 Chendong Pi, Zhang Rou and Sarah Horowitz, 'Fair or Fowl: Industrialization of Poultry Production in China', Institute for Agriculture and Trade Policy, www.iatp.org, 17 February 2014.
3 Mark Godfrey, 'China's "Dragon Head" Seafood Giants Will Drive Next Generation M&A', www.seafoodsource.com, 21 July 2014.
4 'KFC Tightens Control of Chicken Suppliers', www.thepoultrysite.com, 28 March 2013.

5 Mindi Schneider and Shefali Sharma, 'China's Pork Miracle? Agribusiness and Development in China's Pork Industry', Institute for Agriculture and Trade Policy, www.iatp.org, February 2014.
6 Ibid.
7 Sharad Tandon and Maurice Landes, 'India Continues to Grapple with Food Insecurity', Economic Research Service, www.usda.gov, 3 February 2014.
8 Virginia Harrison, 'Holy Cow, India Is the World's Largest Beef Exporter!', *Money*, www.money.cnn.com, 5 August 2015.
9 Abusaleh Sharif, 'Why India Must Not Disrupt Its Balanced Bovine Economy with a Ban on Beef', www.thewire.in, 26 June 2015.
10 Dr T. Kotaiah, 'India's Poultry Market Is Booming', www.thepoultrysite.com, 26 July 2013.
11 Ajay Modi, 'Amazing', *Business Today*, www.businesstoday.in, 25 May 2014.

CONCLUSION

1 'Factory Farming: Assessing Investment Risks', Farm Animal Investment Risk and Return, www.ffair.org, 2016.
2 Eliza Roberts and Brooke Barton, 'Feeding Ourselves Thirsty: How the Food Sector Is Managing Global Water Risks', www.ceres.org, May 2015.
3 'Meat and Animal Feed', www.globalagriculture.org, accessed 2015.

BIBLIOGRAPHY

Abrams, Lindsay, 'How the Meat Industry Killed the Free Market', *Salon*, www.salon.com, 3 March 2014

Adendorff, Lee, 'Life Exports from Australia to Vietnam Skyrocket, But Supply Chain Doubts Remain', *Global Meat News*, www.globalmeatnews.com, 5 March 2015

AFL-CIO, 'Labor Rights in China', www.aflcio.org, 2015

The Agribusiness Accountability Initiative, 'Hogging the Market: How Powerful Meat Packers are Changing our Food System', AAI Issue Brief 4, www.ase.tufts.edu, 2015

Agriculture and Consumer Protection Department, 'Tackling Climate Change through Livestock', Food and Agriculture Organization of the United Nations, www.fao.org, 2015

Agriculture Victoria, 'Code of Accepted Farming Practice for the Welfare of Sheep (Victoria) (Revision Number 2)', agriculture.vic.gov.au, 2015

Aillery, Marcel, Noel Gollehon, Robert Johansson, Jonathan Kaplan, Nigel Key and Marc Ribaudo, 'Managing Manure to Improve Air and Water Quality', *Economic Research Service*, www.ers.usda.gov, 2015

Ainsworth, Claire, and Damian Harrington, 'BSE Disaster: The History', *The New Scientist*, www.newscientist.com, 25 October 2000

Alexandratos, Nikos, and Jelle Bruinsma, 'World Agriculture; Towards 2030/2050, the 2012 Revision', Food and Agriculture Organization of the United Nations, www.fao.org, 2012

Andrews, James, 'Food Fraud a Bigger Problem than Many Realize, Experts Say', *Food Safety News*, www.foodsafetynews.com

Angell Animal Medical Center, 'Farm Animal Welfare: Pigs', The Massachusetts Society for the Prevention of Cruelty to Animals, mspca.org, accessed 2015

Animal Welfare Institute, 'Legal Protections for Farm Animals during Transport', www.awionline.org, accessed 2015

Association de l'Aviculture, de l'Industrie et du Commerce de Volailles dans les Pays de l'Union Européenne, *Annual Report, Association of Poultry Processors and Poultry Trade in the EU Countries*, accessed 2015

The Australian, 'King Island Beef Producers Build their Own Abattoir to Avoid High Fees', www.theaustralian.com.au, 2015

Baldwin, Katherine, and Joanna Bonarriva, 'Feeding the Dragon and the Elephant: How Agricultural Policies and Trading Regimes Influence Consumption in China and India', *Journal of International Commerce and Economics*, www.usitc.gov, May 2013

Balinski, Brent, 'Hockey Approves JBS's $1.4 Billion Takeover of Primo', *Food & Beverage Industry News*, www.foodmag.com.au, 5 March 2015

Barboza, David, 'Meatpackers Profits Hinge on Pool of Immigrant Labor', *New York Times*, www.nytimes.com, 21 December 2001

Barker, James C., 'Frequently Asked Questions about Livestock Production', North Carolina State University, 2015

Beinaert, Jeroen, 'Brazilian Meatpackers Celebrate Landmark Victory on Safety Standards', *Equal Times*, www.equaltimes.org, 7 May 2013

Bhosale, Jayashree, 'Rs 30,000 Crore Buffalo Meat Industry Likely to Stagnate in India This Year', *The Times of India*, www.economictimes.indiatimes.com, 30 October 2015

Birkenstock, Gunther, 'Happy Pork Chops? A New Label for Humane Animal Treatment', *Deutsche Welle*, www.dw.com, 29 October 2012

Biron, Carey L., 'Meatpacking Workers Fight "Unacceptable and Inhumane Conditions"', *MintPress News*, www.mintpressnews.com, 27 March 2014

Bloch, Michael, 'Fast Facts – Meat Consumption Statistics', www.greenlivingtips.com, May 2012

Blount, Jeb, 'BRF Workers in Brazil's Mato Grosso Threaten Strike Over Pay', *Reuters*, www.reuters.com, 14 December 2015

Bric Partner, 'Overview of the Brazilian Poultry Industry', www.bricpartner.com, 2015

Bron, Jan Cees, 'Consolidation in the Meat Industry Continues', *World Poultry*, www.worldpoultry.net, 18 December 2013

Brooks, Cassandra, 'Consequences of Increased Global Meat Consumption on the Global Environment', Stanford Woods Institute for the Environment, www.stanford.edu, 2015

Brown, Lester R., 'Can the World Feed China?', Earth Policy Institute, www.earth-policy.org, 25 February 2014

Bryner, Jeanna, '13 Animal to Human Diseases Kill 2.2 Million People Each Year', www.livescience.com, 6 July 2012

Bunge, Jacob, 'How to Satisfy the World's Surging Appetite for Meat', *Wall Street Journal*, www.wsj.com, 4 December 2015

Byrne, Jane, 'EU Manufacturers Welcome Legal Certainty Medicated Feed Rules Offer', *Feed Navigator*, www.feednavigator.com, 11 September 2014

—, 'Scientists Forecast Massive Hike in Antibiotic Use in Livestock Globally and Call for Legislative Response', *Feed Navigator*, www.feednavigator.com, 24 March 2015

Cai, Lexin, Aidan Pongrace, Christian Butts and Saier Wang, 'China's Astounding Appetite for Pork: Recent Trends and Implications for International Trade', Public Policy Initiative, Penn Wharton, www.wharton.upenn.edu, 2 April 2015

The Cattlesite, 'Asian Demand Influencing World Meat Markets', www.thecattlesite.com, 20 April 2015

Center for Food Security and Public Health, 'National Animal Health Emergency Management System, Foreign Animal Disease Preparedness and Response Plan', Iowa State University, www.cfsph.iastate.edu, October 2014

Centner, T. J., J. C. Alvey and A. M. Stelzleni, 'Beta Agonists in Livestock Feed: Status, Health Concerns, and International Trade', *Journal of Animal Science*, www.ads.uga.edu, XCII (2014), pp. 4234–40

Clements, Mark, 'Asia to Drive 40% of World Poultry Consumption Growth', www.wattagnet.com, 26 May 2015

—, 'Developments in Chinese Poultry Production and Chicken Consumption', www.wattagnet.com, 22 May 2013

Collignon, Peter, and Andreas Voss, 'China, What Antibiotics and What Volumes Are Used in Food Production Animals?', National Institute of Health, www.ncbi.nlm.nih.gov, April 2015

Commonwealth Scientific and Research Organization, 'Animal Hide Washing or Dehairing', www.meatupdate.csiro.au, June 2006
Compa, Lance, 'Blood, Sweat, and Fear: Workers Rights in U.S. Meat and Poultry Plants', Human Rights Watch, www.hrw.org, January 2005
Compassion in World Farming Trust, 'The Welfare of Broiler Chickens in the European Union', www.ciwf.org.uk, 2005
Conniff, Richard, 'Meat Is Murder – But It's People Being Killed (and not how you think)', *Take Part*, www.takepart.com, 6 June 2006
Cook, Rob, 'World Beef Production: Ranking of Countries', Beef2Live.com, 2015
Corah, L. R., 'Development of a Corn-based Beef Industry', Certified Angus Beef LLC, 2015
Costa, L. S., D. F. Pereira, L.G.F. Bueno and H. Pandorfi, 'Some Aspects of Chicken Behavior and Welfare', *Revista Brasileira de Ciência Avícola*, XIV/3, www.scielo.br, May 2012
Costandi, Mo, 'Mad Cows, Cannibalism, and the Shaking Death', *The Guardian*, www.theguardian.com, 26 September 2013
Cotula, Lorenzo, 'Tackling Trade Law Dimension of "Land Grabbing"', International Institute for Environment and Development, www.iied.org, 14 November 2013
—, 'How Investment Treaties Protect Land Grab Deals', Oxfam, www.farmlandgrab.org, 17 February 2016
Curtis, Aerin, 'AFIA Calls for FDA to Roll Back Proposed Species Specific Reporting Requirements', *Feed Navigator*, www.feednavigator.com, 20 August 2015
—, 'Links between Antibiotic Use for Growth Promotion, Cost and Production', *Feed Navigator*, www.feednavigator.com, 15 November 2015
Daley, Erin, 'South America: The World Leader in Exports', *Beef Issues Quarterly*, www.beefissuesquarterly.com, June 2010
Daniels, Jeff, 'Saudi Arabia Buying up Farmland in U.S. Southwest', www.cnbc.com, 15 January 2016
Danovitch, Tove, 'China is Making a Major Play for American Farms and Farmland', *TakePart*, www.takepart.com, 22 February 2016
de Jong, Ingrid, Charlotte Berg, Andy Butterworth and Ina Estevéz, 'Scientific Report Updating the EFSA Opinions on the Welfare of

Broilers and Broiler Breeders', European Food Safety Authority, www.efsa.europa.eu, 2012
Derbyshire, David, 'Arresting Food Fraud', FutureFood2050.com, 18 March 2015
DeWaal, Caroline Smith, and Nadine Robert, 'Food Safety around the World', Concerned Scientists in the Public Interest, www.cspinet.org, June 2005
Duran, Rebeca, 'The Brazilian Cattle Industry', *The Brazil Business*, www.thebrazilbusiness.com, 13 March 2014
Dwyer, Liz, 'What Do Horses and Beavers Have in Common? They May Both Be in Your Burger', *TakePart*, www.takepart.com, 25 August 2015
—, 'Meat Production Statistics', www.ec.europa.eu, 2015
Economic Research Service, 'India's Poultry Sector: Development and Prospects', www.ers.usda.gov, 2015
—, 'Livestock & Meat International Trade Data: Annual and Cumulative Year-to-Date U.S. Livestock and Meat Trade by Country', www.ers.usda.gov, 2015
—, 'Structural Change, Location and Plant Operations', www.ers.usda.gov, 2015
The Economist, 'A Champion for Choice', www.economist.com, 25 August 2012
Elam, Thomas, 'Projections of Global Meat Production through 2050', Center for Global Food Issues, www.farmecon.com, 2015
Elliot, Matthew, 'Beef Market Globalization', *The Angus Journal*, www.angusjournal.com, May 2011
Environmental Protection Agency, 'Nutrient Pollution', www.epa.gov, 2015
European Commission, 'The Meat Sector in the European Union', www.ec.europa.eu, 2004
—, 'Sustainable Development', www.ec.europa.eu, 15 September 2015
—, 'Environment and Agriculture', www.ec.europa.eu, 19 November 2015
—, 'Environmental Crime', www.ec.europa.eu, 19 November 2015
—, 'Animal Health Policy Regulation, Q&A New EU Regulation on Transmissible Animal Diseases', www.ec.europa.eu, March 2016

European Federation of Food, Agriculture and Tourism Trade Unions, 'Zero Tolerance of Labour Exploitation', www.effat.org, 14 December 2015
European Food Information Council, 'European Union Action Plan to Tackle Food Fraud', www.eufic.org, December 2013
European Food Safety Alliance, 'European Food Safety Authority Panel on Animal Health and Welfare (AHAW)', www.efsa.europa.eu, 2012
Eurostat, 'Meat Production Statistics', www.ec.europa.eu, August 2016
Farivar, Cyrus, 'British Scientist Identifies Genetic Sequences in New E-coli Strain', *Deutsche Welle*, www.dw.com, June 2011
—, 'Antibiotic Resistant Chicken Found in German Supermarkets', *Deutsche Welle*, www.dw.com, October 2012
Farmstyle Australia, 'Understanding Cattle Behaviour on Small Farms', farmstyle.com.au, accessed 2015
Fitch, Claire, Robert Martin and Keeve Nachman, 'Limiting Antibiotics Misuse in Food Animals – Legislation We Need', Johns Hopkins Center for a Livable Future blog, www.livablefutureblog.com, 4 March 2016
'Corporate Control in Animal Science Research', *Food and Water Watch*, wwwfoodandwaterwatch.com, April 2015
Food and Agriculture Organization of the United Nations, 'Agriculture's Greenhouse Gas Emissions on the Rise', www.fao.org, 11 April 2014
Food Safety News, www.foodsafetynews.com, 20 August 2015
Fry, John, 'Brazil: Competitive Factors in Brazil Affecting U.S. and Brazilian Agricultural Sales in Selected Third Country Markets', U.S. International Trade Commission, www.usitc.gov, publication 4310, April 2012
Gandhi, Renu, and Suzanne M. Snedeker, 'Consumer Concerns about Hormones in Food', envirocancer.cornell.edu, June 2000
Gao, Mark, 'Meat Industry Is Big Business in China', *Global Meat News*, www.globalmeatnews.com, 15 October 2012
Gerber, P. J., H. Steinfeld, B. Henderson, A. Mottet, C. Opio, J. Dijkman, A. Falcucci and G. Tempio, 'Tackling Climate Change through Livestock – A Global Assessment of Emissions and Mitigation Opportunities', Food and Agriculture Organization of the United Nations, www.fao.org, 2013
Global Agriculture, 'Land Grabbing', www.globalagriculture.org, 2015

GRAIN, 'The Great Food Robbery, How Corporations Control Food, Grab Land, and Destroy the Climate', Fahamu/Pambazuka, 17 May 2012

—, 'Asia's Agrarian Reform in Reverse: Laws Taking Land Out of Smaller Farmer's Hands', www.grain.org, 30 April 2015

—, 'Foreign Pension Funds and Land Grabbing in Brazil', www.grain.org, November 2015

Grant, Rebecca, 'Genetic Testing for Your Hot Dog', *The Atlantic*, www.theatlantic.com, 23 October 2015

Greger, Michael, 'The Long Haul: Risks Associated with Livestock Transport', *Biosecurity and Bioterrorism: Biodefense Strategy, Practice, and Science*, v/4 (2007), pp. 301–11

Gruley, Brian, and Lucia Kassai, 'Brazilian Meatpacker JBS Wrangles the U.S. Beef Industry', www.bloomberg.com, 19 September 2013

Gyton, Georgi, 'Bovine Growth Could Slow for India', *Global Meat News*, www.globalmeatnews.com, 30 June 2015

—, 'Quality, Brand, and Health Sell Meat in Asia', *Global Meat News*, www.globalmeatnews.com, 30 June 2014

—, 'Animal Disease Monitoring Is Critical for Human Health Says FAO', *Global Meat News*, www.globalmeatnews.com, 21 August 2014

—, 'Report Highlights Importance of India as a Global Meat Player', *Global Meat News*, www.globalmeatnews.com, 2 September 2014

—, 'Huge Opportunities in Asian Grocery Markets', www.meatinfo.co.uk, 13 February 2015

Hall, Kevin, 'Modern Day Slavery', *Miami Herald*, www.latinamericanstudies.org, 19 September 2004

Halverson, Nathan, 'U.S. Gives Meat Producers a Pass on Climate Change', *Reveal*, www.revealnews.org, 22 December 2015

Hamel, Gregory, 'The Average Pay of a Meat Packing Worker', *Houston Chronicle*, www.chron.com, 2015

Hamilton, C. R., 'Real and Perceived Issues Involving Animal Protein', Food and Agriculture Organization of the United Nations, www.fao.org, 2015

Han, Siqi, 'Infographic: Environmental Impacts of China's Pork Industry', Wilson Center, www.wilsoncenter.org, 2015

Harrison, Virginia, 'Holy Cow! India Is the World's Largest Beef Exporter', *CNN Money*, www.cnnmoney.com, 5 August 2015

Head, Mike, 'Australian Meat Workers Fight 20% Pay Cut', World Socialist Website, www.wsws.org, 3 June 2013

Heinrich Böll Foundation, 'The Meat Atlas', Friends of the Earth Europe, www.foeeurope.org, 20 January 2014

Hellin, Jon, Vijesh V. Krishna, Olaf Erenstein and Christian Boeber, 'India's Poultry Revolution: Implications for its Sustenance and the Global Poultry Trade', *International Food and Agribusiness Management Review*, www.ifama.org, XVIII, Special Issue A, 2015

Helstocky, Carol, *The SAGE Encyclopedia of Food Issues* (London, 2015), pp. 38–41

Hoffman, David, and Emma Schwartz, 'Sharp Increase Seen in Sales of Antibiotics for Use in Farm Animals', *Frontline*, www.pbs.org, October 2014

Huang, Yanzhong, 'China's Worsening Food Safety Crisis', *The Atlantic*, www.theatlantic.com, 28 August 2012

The Humane Society of the United States, 'An HSUS Report: The Welfare of Animals in the Pig Industry', animalstudiesrepository.org, 2010

—, 'Welfare Issues with Selective Breeding of Egg-laying Hens for Productivity', www.humanesociety.org, 2015

Hutton, Will, 'The Meat Scandal Shows All that is Rotten with our Free Marketeers', *The Guardian*, www.theguardian.com, 16 February 2013

IBISWorld, 'Meat Processing in China: Market Research Report', www.ibisworld.com, December 2015

Jacobson, Brad, 'We Feed Cows Chicken Poop', *Mother Jones*, www.motherjones.com, 19 December 2013

Johnson, Keith, 'Why Is China Spending $43 Billion for a Farming Company?', *Foreign Policy*, www.foreignpolicy.com, 15 February 2016

Kaiman, Jonathan, 'China Arrests 900 in Fake Meat Scandal', *The Guardian*, www.theguardian.com, 3 May 2013

Kaufman, Thomas, 'Sustainable Livestock Production; Low Emission Farm – The Innovative Combination of Nutrient, Emission and Waste Management with Special Emphasis on Chinese Pig Production', *Animal Nutrition*, I/3 (September 2015), pp. 104–12

Kesireddy, Raji Reddy, 'Poultry Market Likely to See Double Digit Growth in 2015', *The Times of India*, *Economic Times*, www.economictimes.indiatimes.com, 25 December 2014

Kesmodel, David, and Laurie Burkitt, 'Inside China's Supersanitary Chicken Farms', *Wall Street Journal*, www.wsj.com, 9 December 2013

Kilgour, Robert J., 'In Pursuit of "Normal": A Review of the Behaviour of Cattle at Pasture', *Science Direct*, www.sciencedirect.com, April 2012

Kinkartz, Sabine, 'The High Cost of Cheap Meat', *Deutsche Welle*, www.dw.com, 1 November 2013

Knight, Cameron, 'Beef Seller in $2M Fraud Case Now Accused of Selling Bad Meat', *The Cincinnati Enquirer*, www.cincinnati.com, 18 November 2015

Knight, Patrick, 'Big Changes in Brazilian Poultry Meat Industry', www.worldpoultry.net, 21 June 2014

Koneswaran, Gowri, and Danielle Nierenberg, 'Global Farm Animal Production and Global Warming: Impacting and Mitigating Climate Change', *Journal of Environmental Health Perspectives*, www.ncbi.nlm.nih,gov, CXVI/5 (May 2008), pp. 578–82

Kotaiah, T., 'India's Poultry Market Is Booming', www.thepoultrysite.com, 26 July 2013

Krieger, Mike, 'Saudi Arabia is Buying up American Farmland to Export Agricultural Products Back Home', *Zero Hedge*, www.zerohedge.com, 17 January 2016

Krishnasamy, Vikram, Joachim Otte and Ellen Silbergeld, 'Antimicrobial Use in Chinese Swine and Broiler Poultry Production', *Antimicrobial Resistance and Infection Control*, www.ncbi.nim.nih, IV/17, 28 April 2015

Kuazaqui, Edmir, Teresinha Covas Lisboa, and Maisa Emilia Raelers Rodrigues, 'A Discussion of Slave Labour at Meatpacking Industries', *Journal of Business and Economics*, VI/3 (March 2015), pp. 468–76

Kuo, Lily, 'The U.S. Meat Processing Company at the Rotten Center of China's Latest Food Scandal', *Quartz*, www.qz.com, 21 July 2014

—, 'The World Eats Cheap Bacon at the Expense of North Carolina's Rural Poor', *Quartz*, www.qz.com, 14 July 2015

Lagos, Joshua Emmanuel, and Vijay Intodia, 'India, Livestock and Products Annual', USDA Foreign Agricultural Services, www.fas.usda.gov, 27 August 2015

Land, Graham, 'Concern is Rising over Meat Consumption in Asia', *Asian Correspondent*, www.asiancorrespondent.com, 27 January 2014
Landes, Maurice, and Kim Hjort, 'Food Policy and Productivity Key to India's Outlook', Economic Research Service, www.ers.usda.gov, 6 July 2015
Lawrence, Felicity, 'Horsemeat Burger Scandal: History Repeating Itself', *The Guardian*, www.theguardian.com, 16 January 2013
Leet, Jessica K., Linda S. Lee, Heather E. Gall, Reuben R. Goforth, Stephen Sassman, Denise A. Gordon, James M. Lazorchak, Mark E. Smith, Chad T. Jafvert and Maria S. Sepúlveda, 'Assessing Impacts of Land-applied Manure from Concentrated Animal Feeding Operations on Fish Populations and Communities', *Environmental Science and Technology*, XLVI/24 (2012), pp. 13440–47
Levin, Simon A., 'Global Trends in Antimicrobial Use in Food Animals', *Proceedings of the National Academy of Sciences*, www.princeton.edu, February 2015
Liu, Pascal, 'Impacts of Foreign Agricultural Investment on Developing Countries: Evidence from Case Studies', Food and Agriculture Organization of the United Nations, www.fao.org, 2014
Livestock Environment and Development, 'China', Food and Agriculture Organization of the United Nations, www.fao.org, 2015
McCarthy, Marty, 'Major Cattle Producer Plays down Concerns about Red Meat Industry Consolidation', www.abc.net.au, 12 November 2015
McGuire, Virginia, 'The Whole World Wants South America's Farmland', *ZDNet*, www.zdnet.com, 12 January 2014
McKenna, Maryn, 'The Abstinence Method', *Modern Farmer*, June 2014
McLendon, Russell, 'How Does the Flu Work?', Mother Nature Network, www.mnn.com, January 2013
McRobert, Katie, 'Hockey Approves JBS Takeover of Primo', *Farm Weekly*, www.farmweekly.com.au, 4 March 2015
Marchant-Forde, Jeremy N., 'Welfare of Sows and Piglets at Farrowing', Economic Research Services, www.usda.gov, 2011
Meat and Livestock Association Australia, 'Hormone Growth Promotants', www.mla.com.au, accessed 2015

—, 'National Livestock Identification System', www.mla.com.au, accessed 2015
The Meat Site, 'Three Quarters of Chicken Test Positive for Campylobacter', www.themeatsite.com, May 2015
—, 'China to Advance Agricultural Modernisation', www.themeatsite.com, 31 December 2015
Meat Tech Asia, 'Meat Tech Asia, Bangalore 2016', www.meattechasia.com, 2016
Meat-workers.org, 'Putting Meat on the Bones: A Report on the Structure and Dynamics of the European Meat Industry', www.meat-workers.org, 2015
Meikle, James, Jemma Buckley and Felicity Lawrence, 'Polish Supplier Linked to Burger Scandal "Had Been Providing Meat for a Year"', *The Guardian*, www.theguardian.com, 30 January 2013
Michigan State University, 'Preventing Food Fraud', *Science Daily*, www.sciencedaily.com, 15 December 2015
Mieszkowski, Katharine, '10 Things to Know before You Eat Your Next Chicken Dinner', *Civil Eats*, www.civileats.com, 7 December 2015
Mills, Elyse, 'Landgrabbing, Conflict and Agrarian–Environmental Transformations: Perspectives from East and Southeast Asia', The Regional Center for Social Science and Sustainable Development, Chiang Mai University, www.iss.nl, May 2015
Minter, Adam, 'Fast Food Loses Its Sizzle in China', *Bloomberg View*, www.bloombergview.com, 22 October 2015
Modi, Ajay, 'In the Pink: Buffalo Meat Exports Thriving under Narendra Modi Government', *Business Today*, www.businesstoday.in, 12 April 2015
—, 'Amazing', *Business Today*, www.businesstoday.in, 25 May 2014
Monbiot, George, 'Toothless Environment Agency is Allowing the Living World to be Wrecked with Impunity', *The Guardian*, www.theguardian.com, 12 November 2015
Moran, John, and Rebecca Doyle, 'Cow Talk, Cattle Behavior', Commonwealth Scientific and Industrial Research Organization, www.csiro.au, February 2015
Morgan, Nancy, 'Meating and Milking the Market: Reviewing Developments in the Livestock Sector', FAO/WorldBank, www.worldbank.org, 2009
Msangi Siwa, Dolapo Enahoro, Mario Herrero, Nicholas Magnan, Petr Havlik, An Notenbaert and Signe Nelgen, 'Integrating

Livestock Feeds and Production Systems into Agricultural Multi-Market Models: The Example of IMPACT', *Science Direct*, www.sciencedirect.com, XLIX Part 2, pp. 365–77, December 2014
Murphy, Sophie, 'Land Grabs and Fragile Food Systems: The Role of Globalization', Institute for Agriculture and Trade Policy, www.iatp.org, February 2013
Nandi, Jayashree, 'India among Top 10 Land Grabbers, Sellers: Report', *The Times of India*, www.timesofindia.com, 27 June 2012
National Chicken Council, 'March Madness – Why Contract Growing in the Chicken Industry is Not a Tournament', www.nationalchickencouncil.org, 15 March 2012
—, 'Vertical Integration: What It Is – Why It's Good for the Chicken Industry . . . and You', www.nationalchickencouncil.org, accessed 2015
National Research Council, Committee on Drug Use in Food Animals, Panel on Animal Health, Food Safety, and Public Health, *The Use of Drugs in Food Animals: Benefits and Risks* (Washington, DC, 1999), p. 31
Natural Resources Defense Council, 'Pollution from Giant Livestock Farms Threatens Public Health', www.nrdc.org, 21 February 2013
Nebehay, Stephanie, 'China's Bird Flu Outbreak Cost $6.5 Billion', *Reuters*, www.reuters.com, 21 May 2013
Nebraska Farmer Goes to Market, 'Translating Food Technology: Why Would Pig Farmers Insist on Using "Gestation Crates?"', nebraska.farmergoestomarket.com, accessed 2015
Nelson, Ken, 'Structural Change in the Meat, Poultry, Dairy, and Grain Processing Industries', Economic Research Service, www.ers.usda.gov, March 2005
North American Meat Institute, 'United States Meat Industry at a Glance', www.meatinstitute.org, 2013
Nuthall, Keith, 'New EU Animal Disease Law Combines Vigilance with Sensitivity to Antimicrobial Resistance', *Global Meat News*, www.globalmeatnews.com, 3 June 2015
O'Donaghue, Jasmine, 'Meat Industry Moves toward Consolidation', *Food & Beverage Industry News*, www.foodmag.com.au, 8 July 2015
O'Leary, Patrick, 'Neoliberal Employer Industrial Relations Strategies in the U.S. and Australian Meat Industries', Business School at the University of Ballarat, Australia, www.vu.edu.au, 2012

Oenema, Oene, 'Livestock Production and Manure Management in EU 27', Wageningen University, www.reusewaste.eu, 2012
Oldroyd, Rachel, 'Who Owns the Planet?', The Bureau of Investigative Journalism, www.thebureauinvestigates.com, 30 May 2012
Olivier, Shar, 'CAFOs as Hotspots: Effect on Ecosystem Services and Needed Change in Environmental Leadership', http://dukespace.lib.duke.edu, May 2012
Ollinger, Michael, Sang V. Nguyen, Donald Blayney, Bill Chambers and Ken Nelson, 'Structural Change in the Meat, Poultry, Dairy, and Grain Processing Industries', Economic Research Service, www.ers.usda.gov, March 2005
Om, Jason, 'Foreign Workers Exploited at Baiada Chicken Processing Plants: Fair Work Ombudsman Finds', www.abc.net.au, 17 June 2015
Oxfam, 'Our Land, Our Lives', www.oxfam.org, October 2012
—, 'Still Banking on Land Grabs: Australia's Four Big Banks and Land Grabs', www.farmlandgrab.org, 15 February 2016
Oxfam America, 'Lives on the Line, The Human Cost of Cheap Chicken', www.oxfamamerica.org, October 2015
Parliamentary Offices of Science and Technology, 'Livestock Disease', POST No. 392, www.ifst.org, October 2011
Perkowski, Jack, 'China's Growing Food Problem/Opportunity', *Forbes*, www.forbes.com, 25 September 2014
Pi, Chendong, Zhang Rou and Sarah Horowitz, 'Fair or Fowl: Industrialization of Poultry Production in China', Institute for Agriculture and Trade Policy, www.iatp.org, 17 February 2014
Pighills, Thomas, 'Globalization and the Meat Industry', *Prezi*, www.prezi.com, 9 May 2015
The Poultry Site, 'Major Poultry Producing Countries', www.thepoultrysite.com, August 2007
—, 'Poultry Sold as Veal: Report Reveals Dishonest Labeling', www.thepoultrysite.com, 6 November 2015
Powell, Doug, 'Food Fraud: Mutton Isn't Lamb, Abattoir Convicted of Large-scale Lamb Substitution', www.barfblog.com, 1 February 2013
—, 'Look Harder, There's More Fraud: Fake-food Scandal Revealed as UK Tests Show Third of Products Mislabeled', www.barfblog.com, 10 February 2014

—, 'Food Fraud: 20% Samples Had Undeclared Meat in UK Lamb Takeaway Survey', www.barfblog.com, 9 February 2015
—, 'Food Fraud: Record Seizures of Fake Food and Drink in INTERPOL–Europol Operation', www.barfblog.com, 22 February 2015
—, 'Let Them Eat Ass, Say Egypt's Food Safety Officials', www.barfblog.com, 23 June 2015
—, 'Food Fraud Nothing New: But We Will Survive', www.barfblog.com, 7 November 2015
—, 'Food Fraud: U.S. Man Faces 5 Years for False Claim that Beef Was Free of *E. coli*', www.barfblog.com, 9 November 2015
—, 'Hit Fraudsters Where It Hurts: Cash Flow', www.barfblog.com, 8 December 2015
—, 'Food Fraud: Ton of Meat Seized by Food Safety Officers from Halal Butchers in Glasgow', www.barfblog.com, 27 January 2016
The Press and Journal, 'Chicken Farmer Exits Sector as Processor Restructures', www.pressandjournal.co.uk, 1 March 2014
Productivity Commission, 'Work Arrangements in the Australian Meat Processing Industry', www.pc.gov.au, 1990
Regional Office for Asia and the Pacific, 'Vertical Integration and the Livestock Industries of the Asia-Pacific Region', Food and Agriculture Organization of the United Nations, www.fao.org, 2015
Renner, Michael, 'Peak Meat Production Strains Land and Water Resources', Worldwatch Institute, www.worldwatch.org, August 2014
Reuver, Marieke, 'Sub-regional Report on Animal Genetic Resources: Southeast Asia', Annex to The State of the World's Animal Genetic Resources for Food and Agriculture, Food and Agriculture Organization of the United Nations, www.fao.org, 2007
Rice, Alison, 'Congress Shivers at $1 Billion Tariff Threat, Kills COOL', *Drovers*, www.cattlenetwork.com, 18 December 2015
Rice, Christina, 'What's in Your Food? A Look at Food Fraud', *Food Safety News*, www.foodsafetynews.com, 14 April 2015
Roberts, Dexter, 'Soaring Meat Production Threatens Global Environment, Warns Report', *Bloomberg*, www.bloomberg.com, 27 August 2014
Robertson, Joshua, 'Beef, Big Bucks, and Buy Ups: Are Chinese Investors Changing the Face of Australia?', *The Guardian*, www.theguardian.com, 6 August 2015

Rodrigo, Pooma, 'EU Meat Exports to Vietnam Surge', *Global Meat News*, www.globalmeatnews.com, 20 May 2015
Rose-Smith, Imogen, 'Institutional, Impact Investing Find Common Ground in Agriculture', *Institutional Investor*, www.institutionalinvestor.com, 16 January 2015
Rousseau, Oscar, 'Bord Bia's New Carbon Target for Beef', *Global Meat News*, www.globalmeatnews.com, 10 November 2015
—, 'BRF in $50 Million Takeover of Universal Meats', *Global Meat News*, www.globalmeatnews.com, 4 February 2016
Rowe, Mark, 'Meat Industry Must Lobby to Protect Interests after Paris Climate Change Deal', *Global Meat News*, www.globalmeatnews.com, 16 December 2016
Rueter, Gero, 'Berlin Targets Superbugs in Animal Feed', *Deutsche Welle*, www.dw.com, September 2012
Ruiz, Benjamin, 'The Advance of the Brazilian Poultry Industry', www.wattagnet.com, 7 February 2014
Rural Migration News, 'Meat and Migrants', *Rural Migration News*, XX/1 (January 2014), migration.ucdavis.edu
Ryan, Chloe, 'U.S. Funds Pandemic Animal Disease Action', *Global Meat News*, www.globalmeatnews.com, 22 October 2015
Santo, Raychel, 'New FAO Report on Livestock and Climate Change, Johns Hopkins Center for a Livable Future blog, www.livablefutureblog.com, 15 October 2013
Schneider, Mindi, and Shefali Sharma, 'China's Pork Miracle? Agribusiness and Development in China's Pork Industry', Institute for Agriculture and Trade Policy, www.iatp.org, February 2014
Scott, Kylene, 'Global Beef Trade Picture Challenging', *High Plains Journal*, www.hpj.com, 12 January 2016
Seeking Alpha, 'Meat Companies Earning their Pound of Flesh', www.seekingalpha.com, 21 January 2016
Sharma, Shefali, 'The Need for Feed: China's Demand for Industrialized Meat and Its Impacts', Institute for Agriculture and Trade Policy, www.iatp.org, 17 February 2014
Sheffi, Yossi, 'The Power of Resilience: How the Best Companies Manage the Unexpected', *MIT Press*, 11 September 2015
Shell, Ellen Rupell, 'Could Mad Cow Disease Happen Here?', *The Atlantic*, www.theatlantic.com, September 1999

Shih, Toh Han, 'China's Demand for Meat to Change the Face of Global Trade in Feed Grains', *South China Morning Post*, www.scmp.com, 2015

Smith, Cynthia P., 'Information Resources on the Care and Welfare of Beef Cattle', United States Department of Agriculture, www.usda.gov, June 2004

Smith, P., M. Bustamante, H. Ahammad, H. Clark, H. Dong, E. A. Elsiddig, H. Haberl, R. Harper, J. House, M. Jafari, O. Masera, C. Mbow, N. H. Ravindranath, C. W. Rice, C. Robledo Abad, A. Romanovskaya, F. Sperling and F. Tubiello, 'Agriculture, Forestry and Other Land Use', *Contribution of Working Group III to the Fifth Assessment Report of the Intergovernmental Panel on Climate Change*, www.ipcc.ch, 2014

Sommer, Ron, 'Where's the Beef? Consolidation in the Meat Processing Industry', www.seekingalpha.com, 25 June 2014

Spotts, Pete, 'How Brazilian Beef Industry Became Latest Ally in Fight against Deforestation', *Christian Science Monitor*, www.csmonitor.com, 12 May 2015

Starmer, Elanor, 'Environmental and Health Problems in Livestock Production', The Agribusiness Accountability Initiative, www.ase.tufts.edu, 2015

Steiner, Rupert, 'No Hen Party for Suffering UK Poultry Firms as Producers Struggle to Make Ends Meet', www.thisismoney.co.uk, 4 March 2013

Steinfeld, Henning, 'Livestock's Long Shadow', Food and Agricultural Organization of the United Nations, www.fao.org, 2006

Stone, Judy, 'New Superbug Resistant to All Antibiotics Linked to Imported Meat', *Forbes*, www.forbes.com, 12 December 2015

Tan, Gillian, 'Morgan Stanley Lines up Behind Tyson', *Wall Street Journal*, www.wsj.com, 29 May 2014

Tandon, Sharad, and Maurice Landes, 'India Continues to Grapple with Food Insecurity', Economic Research Service, www.usda.gov, 3 February 2014

Tanoue, Rumi, Yuri Sato, Miki Motoyama, Shuhei Nakagawa, Ryota Shinohara and Kei Nomiyama, 'Plant Uptake of Pharmaceutical Chemicals Detected in Recycled Organic Manure and Reclaimed Wastewater', *Journal of Agricultural Food Chemistry*, LX/41 (24 September 2012), pp 10203–11

Tavener, Ben, 'Responsible u.s. Pension Fund Invested in Brazil Farmland Seized by Violent Land-grabbers', *Vice News*, bentavener.com, 18 November 2015

Teenstra, E., T. Vellinga, N. Aektasaeng, W. Amatayakul, A. Ndambi, D. Pelster, L. Germer, A. Jenet, C. Opio and K. Andeweg, 'Global Assessment of Manure Management Policies and Practices', Wageningenur University, www.wageningenur.nl, December 2014

Ter Beek, Vincent, 'Renewed Focus on Finishers in Denmark', *Pig Progress*, www.pigprogress.com, 18 December 2015

Thorne, Peter S., 'Environmental Health Impacts of Concentrated Animal Feeding Operations: Anticipating Hazards – Searching for Solutions', *Environmental Health Perspectives*, www.ncbi.nim.gov, cxv/2 (February 2007), pp. 296–329

The United Food and Commercial Workers International Union, 'Packing and Processing', www.ufcw.org, 2015

United States Department of Agriculture, 'Quarterly Enforcement Report July 1, 2015 through September 30, 2015', www.usda.gov, 2015

United States Food and Drug Administration, 'Steroid Hormone Implants Used for Growth in Food-producing Animals', www.fda.gov, 20 October 2015

—, 'Feed Ban Enhancement: Implementation Questions and Answers, Bovine Spongiform Encephalopathy', www.fda.gov, 2015

United States International Trade Commission, 'Brazil: Competitive Factors in Brazil Affecting u.s. and Brazilian Agricultural Sales in Selected Third Country Markets', www.usitc.gov, publication 4310, April 2012

United States Poultry and Egg Association, 'The Real Truth about Chicken', www.realtruthaboutchicken.com, 2013

Valente, Marcela, 'Curbing Foreign Ownership of Farmland', Al Jazeera, www.aljazeera.com, 22 May 2011

Wade, Louise Carroll, 'Meatpacking', *Encyclopedia of Chicago*, www.encyclopedia.chicagohistory.org, 2005

Wagner, Bettina, and Anke Hassel, 'Labor Migration and the German Meat Processing Industry: Fundamental Freedoms and the Influx of Cheap Labor, *South Atlantic Quarterly*, cxiv(1) (January 2015)

Waldie, Paul, 'Boardroom Farmers: Some of the World's Biggest Agricultural Investors', *The Globe and Mail*, www.theglobeandmail.com, 24 November 2010

—, and Jessica Leeder, 'Do Corporate Buyouts Signal the End of the Family Farm?', *The Globe and Mail*, www.theglobeandmail.com, 24 November 2010
Washington State Department of Health, 'Animal Transmitted Diseases', www.doh.wa.gov, 2015
Wasley, Andrew, 'UK Chicken Farming Puts Workers and Food Safety at Risk', *The Guardian*, www.theguardian.com, 22 December 2015
The Weekly Times, 'Meat Consolidation to Increase', www.weeklytimesnow.au, 9 May 2014
Wegener, Henrik, 'Antibiotic Resistance – Linking Human and Animal Health', National Center for Biotechnology Information, bookshelf # NBK114485, www.ncbi.nim.nlh.gov, 2012
Weiss, Regina, 'Ninety Years On – Will the Feds Finally Break Up the Meat Monopoly?', *Huffington Post*, www.huffingtonpost.com, 30 August 2010
White, Victoria, 'Food Fraud: Lessons from the Horsemeat Scandal', *New Food Magazine*, www.newfoodmagazine.com, 12 January 2016
Whittaker, William G., 'Labor Practices in the Meatpacking and Poultry Processing Industry', *CRS Report for Congress*, www.nationalaglawcenter.org, 20 July 2005
Wiehoff, Dale, 'Where Have All the Dead Chickens Gone?', Institute for Agriculture and Trade Policy, www.iatp.org, 26 August 2015
Wilkie, Rhoda M., *Livestock/Deadstock: Working with Farm Animals from Birth to Slaughter* (Philadelphia, PA, 2010)
World Animal Protection, 'Recognizing Animal Protection', api.worldanimalprotection.org, 2014
World Health Organization, 'Tackling Antibiotic Resistance from a Food Safety Perspective', www.euro.who.int, 2011
World Poultry, 'Four Countries Receive Highest Animal Welfare Rating', www.pigprogress.net, 10 December 2014
Worldwatch Institute, 'China Embraces Meat Safety Legislation', www.worldwatch.org, 2013
—, 'Meat Production Continues to Rise', www.worldwatch.org, 2015
Yusupov, Adel, 'Southeast Asia: A Rapidly Modernizing Economic Powerhouse', U.S. Grains Council, www.grains.org, 19 June 2014
Zonca, Craig, 'Unprecedented Demand Driving Strong Competition for Australian Farmland', www.abc.net.au, 20 January 2016

ACKNOWLEDGEMENTS

My thanks first and foremost to Patrick Martins and the Heritage Radio Network for giving me the platform and the opportunity to learn about the food system in general and the meat industry in particular. My thanks to my various readers, most notably Sylvia Falcon and Charles Hayes, as well as Rose Marie Morse and Charles Keiffer. Andy Smith provided invaluable advice on putting this project together. Lastly my thanks go to those in the meat industry who opened their doors, allowed me to view their processes and answered my many questions.

INDEX

animal welfare 31, 72–6, 81–6, 90–91, 127, 163
antibiotic resistance 18, 47, 49, 63
antibiotics 17–18, 21–3, 53–5, 83, 149, 156, 163–5
antimicrobial resistance 20
  see also multi-drug-resistant (MDR) pathogens 19, 21–3, 53–4, 62
avian flu 24, 41–3
  AI 42
  HPAI H5N1 43

beta-agonists 83–5, 156, 162
biosecurity 32
Bovine Spongiform Encephalopathy (BSE) 38, 40–41, 51
  see also Creutzfeld-Jakob Disease and vCreutzfeld-Jakob Disease
Brasil Foods 8, 146
Brown, Lester 143

CAFO 12–16, 17, 22–8, 47, 58–9, 60–63, 151, 163–6
Campylobacter 21–2, 49, 55, 62, 87, 125
Campylobacteriosis 44, 51, 55
Cargill 8, 17, 25, 105, 112, 134, 158, 162–6
Centers for Disease Control (CDC) 23, 42
Chan, Dr Margaret 20
Con Agra 14
Consumer Reports 21, 53
Consumers Union 127
Country of Origin Labeling (COOL) 125–7
Creutzfeld-Jakob Disease and vCreutzfeld-Jakob Disease (CJD and VCJD) 39–40

E. coli 21, 22, 44–9, 52–7, 62, 66, 87, 165
European Food Safety Authority (EFSA) 55–6

Five Freedoms 72, 73, 75
Fleming, Alexander 17
Food and Agriculture Organization of the United Nations (FAO) 21, 58, 63–9
foot and mouth disease 113

Grandin, Dr Temple 88–91, 99

heritage breeds 28, 34
heterosis 27
Hormel 15
hybrid vigour 27, 29

integrator 15, 107–12

JBS 8, 15, 25, 105, 111–13, 132, 161
Jewel, Jesse 13

Leonard, Christopher 108
Listeria 51, 56, 62, 66
Listeriosis 44–5, 51, 56
Livestock's Long Shadow 69

Monfort, Warren 14
Moss, Michael 31
Moy Park 18, 134
MRSA (methicillin-resistant
Staphylococcus aureus) 23, 56

National Antimicrobial
Resistance Monitoring
System (NARMS) 18
National Beef Packing 15
National Pork Producers
Council 16

OIE (World Organization for
Animal Health) 74
Oxfam 135

Perdue 15, 162
Pilgrim's Pride 15

Rangan, Dr Urvashi 21

Salmonella 21–2, 45, 51–6, 62, 66,
87, 125, 165
Salmonellosis 44, 52–3, 56
Sanderson 15
Smithfield 8, 24, 77, 132–7, 141–8,
150, 163
SVF Foundation 35
swine flu 41, 42
H1N1 42

Tyson 8, 15, 24–5, 105–9, 112,
146–9, 161–2
Tyson, John 13

U.S. Department of Agriculture
(USDA) 87–9, 100, 129
U.S. Food and Drug
Administration (FDA) 18,
19, 85

vertical integration 15, 26,
105–10, 161
Vion 18

WH Group 8, 15, 77, 132–3, 141
World Animal Protection
Organization 73–4, 90
World Health Organization
(WHO) 20–22, 44, 52, 56, 63
Wrangham, Richard 11

Yum! Brands 145, 149